Pearson's Railway

THE CUMBRIAN C

Published by J.M. Pearson & Son,
Tatenhill Common, Staffordshire DE13 9RS.
Telephone: (0283) 713674.

©Michael Pearson. All Rights Reserved.
First edition 1992. ISBN 0 907864 61 9.

Cartography by Malcolm Barnes of Burton upon Trent.
Illustrations by Eric Leslie.
Typesetting by Sprint Typesetting & Artwork of
Burton upon Trent.
Printed by Penwell Print of Callington, Cornwall.

Introduction

If the father of railways, George Stephenson, had got his way, the coastal route would have been the main line to Scotland, and the story of this backwater branchline would have been markedly different. Instead it was built in instalments by a farrago of independent and semi-independent railway companies whose *rationale* was to profit from the rich mineral deposits of West Cumbria. The route round the coast was complete by 1857 and subsequent take-overs and amalgamations brought the line within the control of three companies: the Furness Railway; the London & North Western; and the Maryport & Carlisle.

For sixty years the three railways experienced fluctuating levels of profit and loss, largely commensurate with the boom times and depressions of local industry. The Maryport & Carlisle was the most consistently successful, the Furness flourished fitfully and, as far as the London & North Western was concerned, its West Cumbrian lines were of marginal interest; an *ultima Thule* far removed from the importance of Euston, Crewe and Carlisle.

It was the Furness Railway who flirted with tourism. By the turn of the nineteenth century, revenue from the carriage of iron ore upon which the fortunes of the railway had largely been based, was declining and the company was seeking to encourage extra passengers as an alternative means of income. It strove to make the most of its location on the coastal fringe of the Lake District. Branches were built to Lake Windermere and Coniston Water and, by virtue of connecting services with the Midland Railway at Carnforth, and a steamer service across Morecambe Bay from Fleetwood, holiday-makers were tempted to make their approach to the Lakes by way of the Furness Railway's routes.

Not that the coast was entirely ignored. The Furness Railway had two attempts at creating seaside resorts at Grange-over-Sands and Seascale. They succeeded on a modest scale at the former, though it never seriously held up to their claim to be 'the Bournemouth of the North'. But the latter soon faded into obscurity, being perhaps too remote and too windswept to attract families intent on the enjoyment of a traditional seaside holiday.

All three railways were absorbed into the London Midland & Scottish system in 1923. The bigger company, with interests stretching from London to the northern tip of Scotland, and including much of Wales, had better established tourist areas to promote than the remote fringes of Lancashire and Cumberland. Similarly British Railways, who took control at the beginning of 1948, were also preoccupied with more obviously attractive resorts, and the Cumbrian Coast railway lanquished as a local line concerned uppermost with a fragmentary and diminishing commuter traffic.

GREEN ROAD

"FURNESS FLYER" AT MEATHOP

So much then for the history of the Cumbrian Coast railway, but what does it have to offer present day travellers? Its character is now very much that of a secondary by-way. A small amount of freight still uses the line, notably the nuclear flask traffic to Sellafield and a modicum of opencast coal from Maryport, but the majority of trains on the line are 'Sprinter' type diesel units carrying passengers. Given the indented nature of the coastline, and the lack of esturial road crossings, the railway more than holds its own in the face of the sort of road transport competition that has undermined railways in busier parts of the country, and most rail users on the Cumbrian Coast line are travelling on business (in the loosest sense of the term) as opposed to pleasure. Such a proportional balance in favour of the everyday traveller sustains the railway's character, so that the visitor senses a welcome reality and purpose about the trains in place of the phoney ambience prevalent on more tourist orientated lines.

Rolling stock apart, modernisation has largely eluded the Cumbrian Coast railway. Much of its infrastructure harks back to an earlier, less technological era of railway operation. Mechanical signal boxes still oversee 'block' sections of line and progress is guarded by traditional semaphore signalling. Level crossings abound, many still conventionally gated and operated by hand. A feeling of community permeates the railwaymen and women who work on the line, and a common bond links the drivers, guards, station staff, signalmen and plate-layers at one end of the line with their counterparts at the other. A job of work it may be, but one senses a possessive pride in the service that their efforts gell together to provide.

It is to be hoped that publication of this guide will engender more interest and travel on the railway it describes. The old axim of 'use it or lose it' still hangs over the line in the 1990s as the railway system heads towards the uncertainties, if not the opportunities of privatisation. It would be difficult to see how public transport could be provided more effectively in the region either geographically or environmentally. But there are those in the skirting boards of the corridors of power for whom the watchword of bottom line accountancy carries more clout than that of public service, and in a world where money talks the railway round the Cumbrian Coast needs all the listeners it can muster.

HARRINGTON HARBOUR

Using this Guide

Thirteen inch to a mile, north facing maps portray the route of the Cumbrian Coast railway from Lancaster to Carlisle. These are accompanied by a running commentary on the course of the line and the landscape it passes through. Emphasis is given to the northward journey, but the details are equally relevant for travel in the opposite direction.

The commentary concentrates on describing the course of the railway and on discussing points of associated interest. For further details of the places served by the line, turn to the gazetteer. This, along with a brief portrait of the character of each settlement, includes details of suggested places of refreshment and (where appropriate) accommodation, shopping facilties, and a resumé of lesiure activities. Please note however that facilities of this sort are susceptible to change, and the advice of the local Tourist Information Centre should be sought where accuracy is essential.

Interspersed with the main text and maps are a number of 'mini-features', mostly describing walks from stations along the line. These are presented in the 'first person' for the sake of atmosphere, and are intended to encourage readers to concoct their own walking itineraries along and beside the Cumbrian Coast railway.

When to Go

Railway journeys can be rewarding at any time of the year. Out of season, tourist haunts (and the trains which serve them) tend to be quieter and more revealing of the charms since sacrificed to popularity The landscapes (and seascapes) of the Cumbrian Coast change appearance with the seasons, and there is just as much enjoyment to be derived from a winter journey on the line, when the grey waves of the Irish Sea are crashing down on the coastline, as in the summer when the sea is (supposed to be) blue and calm and inviting.

By and large, Cumbrian Coast trains don't suffer from the sort of overcrowding experienced during the peak tourist season by the neighbouring Settle & Carlisle line. In all our research trips on the line, the only services we came upon to be consistently busy were the 'nine o'clock' departure from Barrow to Lancaster and the 'teatime' departures from Sellafield, crammed with BNFL workers.

Acknowledgements

The publishers extend grateful thanks to all the staff of British Rail and Regional Railways who helped with the compilation of this guide, especially Geoff Holme of Barrow who spent a day guiding us over the line and Stephen Cornish of Manchester who gave us much insight into current policy.

The maps were produced from OS 6″ base material 1909-38 updated by personal survey. Gradient figures were provided by B.R. at Carnforth - thanks to Ian Gorton & Co.

Thanks, as always, to all at Penwell, to Malcolm Barnes and Eric Leslie, to Andrew and Heather at Sprint Typesetting & Artwork, and to everyone else involved with the production and marketing of this title.

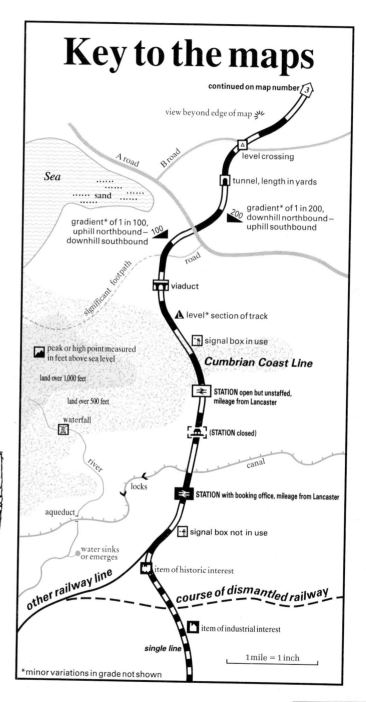

Key to the maps

continued on map number 3

view beyond edge of map

A road B road

Sea

sand

gradient* of 1 in 100, uphill northbound – downhill southbound 100

level crossing

tunnel, length in yards

gradient* of 1 in 200, downhill northbound – uphill southbound 200

road

significant footpath

viaduct

level* section of track

signal box in use

peak or high point measured in feet above sea level

land over 1,000 feet

Cumbrian Coast Line

land over 500 feet

waterfall

STATION open but unstaffed, mileage from Lancaster

(STATION closed)

river

canal

locks

STATION with booking office, mileage from Lancaster

aqueduct

signal box not in use

water sinks or emerges

item of historic interest

other railway line

course of dismantled railway

item of industrial interest

single line

1 mile = 1 inch

*minor variations in grade not shown

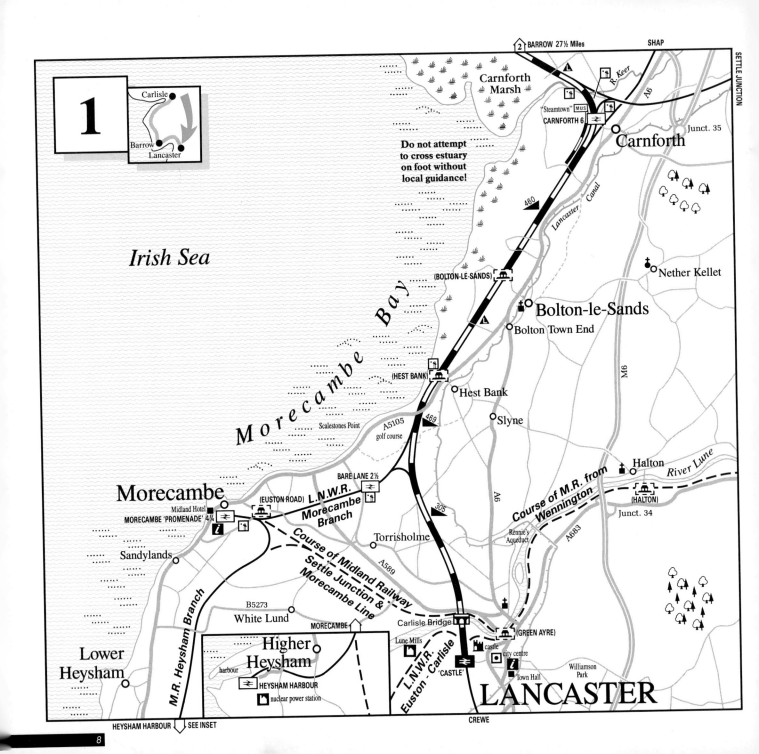

1

Carlisle

Barrow
Lancaster

BARROW 27½ Miles · **2** · SHAP

Carnforth Marsh

Irish Sea

Do not attempt
to cross estuary
on foot without
local guidance!

"Steamtown" MUS

CARNFORTH 6

Carnforth

Junct. 35

Lancaster Canal

460

Nether Kellet

(BOLTON-LE-SANDS)

Bolton-le-Sands

Bolton Town End

M o r e c a m b e   B a y

M6

(HEST BANK)

Hest Bank

Slyne

Scalestones Point

A5105
golf course

469

Halton

River Lune

Course of M.R. from Wennington

(HALTON)

Junct. 34

BARE LANE 2½

Morecambe

(EUSTON ROAD) **L.N.W.R.**

Midland Hotel

MORECAMBE 'PROMENADE' 4¼

Morecambe Branch

Torrisholme

A6

A5589

305

Rennie's
Aqueduct

A683

Sandylands

Course of Midland Railway
Settle Junction &
Morecambe Line

B5273

White Lund

MORECAMBE

**Higher
Heysham**

HEYSHAM HARBOUR

nuclear power station

Carlisle Bridge

Lune Mills

(GREEN AYRE)

castle
city centre

**Lower
Heysham**

M.R. Heysham Branch

harbour

L.N.W.R. Euston - Carlisle 'CASTLE'

Town Hall

Williamson
Park

LANCASTER

SETTLE JUNCTION

R. Keer

A6

HEYSHAM HARBOUR · SEE INSET

CREWE

IF INTERCITY have deposited you with time to spare before the Regional Railways service departs for the Cumbrian Coast, don't kill that time in the fuggy warmth of the waiting room, saunter instead around the precincts of the station. Lancaster is a city famous for its beautiful and historic buildings, and the railway station is no exception. Dating from 1846, it was designed for the Lancaster & Carlisle Railway by Sir William Tite, who took as his architectural theme, the towers and turrets of the adjoining medieval castle. Indeed, until Beeching went and closed Lancaster's other station at 'Green Ayre', this was known as 'Castle' station, and one imagines that less well informed passengers were under the impression that the railway builders had laid their tracks through the original fortress, converting the great hall into a ticket office, and keeping the left luggage in the dungeon.

Lancaster station wears its age well. The mellow stone walls have resisted modernisation as the castle walls resisted the Scots. To accommodate increasing services, extensions were added in 1858 and 1900, but they were executed in harmony with Tite's original, and you would need to know your valance from your voussoir to be able to discern the joins. Glance at your watch and judge how long you have left, because there is something no departure for the Cumbrian Coast should be made without seeing first. In the entrance passage on the west side of the station stand a pair of glass display cases. One contains a very fine scale model of the Isle of Man ferry *King Orry* built at Birkenhead in 1913. The other, coincidentally, dates from the same year and is a plaster cast relief map of the Lake District, showing all but the northern section of the Cumbrian Coast railway. If adrenalin for the journey ahead is not already overflowing, this gorgeous model will clinch it; those old railway publicity departments certainly knew their stuff. Now off you go and catch the Barrow train.

As far as Carnforth, Cumbrian Coast trains run 'under the wires' of the West Coast Main Line, and the 'Sprinters' which provide most of the Barrow and Cumbrian Coast services have to put their best foot forward to slot in with the Scottish expresses. Almost immediately the line crosses high above the River Lune on a bridge originally designed by Joseph Locke. Railway travellers are treated to a grandstand glimpse of the river sweeping out towards the sea past the remnants of Lancaster's once flourishing maritime past. Upstream, the former Midland Railway's crossing of the Lune has been rebuilt as a road bridge. Almost seventy years before the main line was electrified in the early Seventies, the Midland Railway experimented with electric traction on their Lancaster to Morecambe and Heysham line.

Accelerating away from the suburbs, northbound trains pass the triangular junction of the branch to Morecambe and Heysham. Nowadays a fairly regular shuttle service of trains links Lancaster with the coastal resort of Morecambe, but only two trains a day run on to Heysham for ferry passengers to and from the Isle of Man. Morecambe's railway history is quite complex, and though it is the Midland Railway's 'Promenade' station to which trains run now, it is the tracks of the London & North Western which take them there. Why not earmark exploration of the branch for another day?

Meanwhile, back on the main line, at Hest Bank, the sea comes into view for the only time on the misleadingly known West *Coast* Main Line; and even then, if the tide has ebbed its way across the wide sands of Morecambe Bay, the briney itself well may be out of sight. A mile to the east of Bolton-le-Sands the M6 motorway strides over the neighbouring ridge impervious to the contours of the hills. Three older lines of communication - the canal, the A6 and the railway - are squeezed, however, on to the coastal plain to avoid the need for time consuming gradients. The Lancaster Canal once stretched all the way from Preston to Kendal, but nowadays only 46 miles remain open for pleasure boating, the northern terminus lying just beyond Carnforth. Before the motorway opened the A6 was everybody's nightmarish route to The Lakes and Scotland. Now it is relatively quiet, and towns like Lancaster and Carnforth are the better for it.

Ten minutes after leaving Lancaster the brakes go on for the approach to CARNFORTH and the start of the Cumbrian Coast rail experience proper. Though not necessarily being aware of it, millions of post war cinema goers would recognise Carnforth station cafeteria from its use in the film "Brief Encounter". You know, the David Lean weepy where Trevor Howard and Celia Johnson make stiff-upper-lipped love over plates of railway rockbuns to the strains of Rachmaninov's second piano concerto. The cafeteria closed long ago - presumably there weren't enough dewy-eyed couples to make it pay - but a plaque recalls its use as a film set.

If Carnforth's railway kindles one set of emotions in movie buffs, it registers quite differently on the Richter Scale of railway enthusiasm, for the motive power depot here remained operative right up until the official end of steam on British Rail in 1968. Furthermore, its survival as a centre for the maintenance and display of preserved steam locomotives, under the name of "Steamtown", ensures that a steady stream of revivalist steam fans continue to make a pilgrimmage to Carnforth. Though one senses that too many of them do so by road.

In common with Lancaster, Carnforth station deserves more than a cursory glance. It developed as a meeting point of three companies prior to the railway grouping of 1923. The London & North Western operated the main line, the Midland Railway came in from West Yorkshire over their line - jointly owned with the Furness Railway from Wennington - and the Furness itself ran services around the coast to Barrow and beyond. Archive photographs show what a handsome and busy station Carnforth must have been. Prior to 1938 the branch line platform was spanned by an elegant overall roof, but the LMS demolished this when they built a second platform for the Barrow line with a concrete awning in contemporary 'art deco' style. The main line pair of platforms were taken out of use in the Sixties, rendering it impossible to arrive from the North unless travelling by the roundabout coastal route from Carlisle.

Wheels squealing round the tight curves, the Barrow train pulls away from Carnforth at the beginning of its coastal odyssey. To the west there are glimpses of 'Steamtown's nostalgic array of locomotives and rolling stock, to the east sidings of yellow and grey liveried engineering wagons shunted by similarly painted class 31 and 47 diesels, for Carnforth is a centre for track maintenance. Crossing the little River Keer, which rises in the hilly district around Kirkby Lonsdale, the railway moves out into a marshland landscape which sets the tone for the next leg of the journey around the edge of Morecambe Bay to Ulverston.

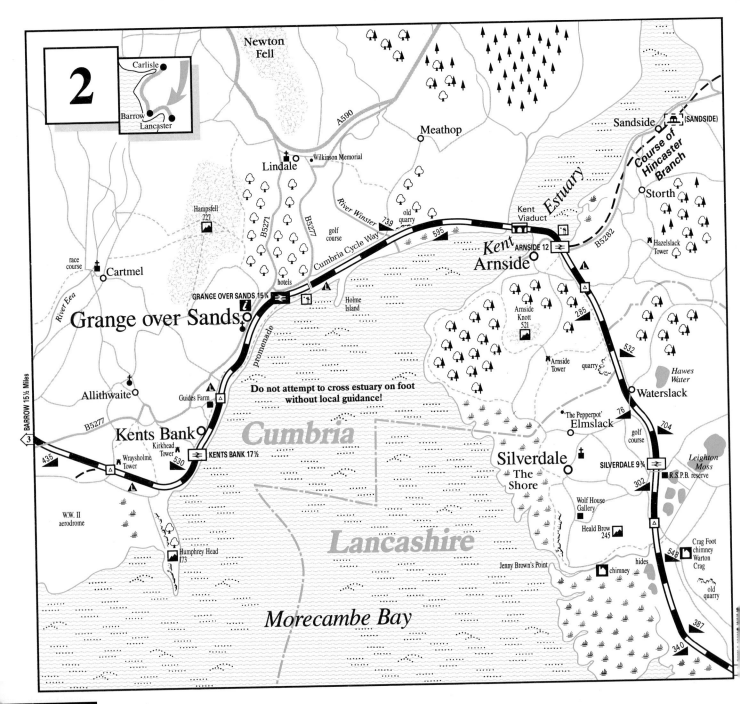

2

Carlisle
Barrow
Lancaster

Newton Fell

A590

Meathop

Wilkinson Memorial

Lindale

River Winster

739

old quarry

Kent Viaduct

Estuary

Course of Hincaster Branch

Sandside (SANDSIDE)

Storth

B5282

Hazelslack Tower

Hampsfell 727

B5271   B5277

golf course

Cumbria Cycle Way

595

Kent

ARNSIDE 12

Arnside

race course

Cartmel

hotels

GRANGE OVER SANDS 15¾

Holme Island

Arnside Knott 521

285

532

Hawes Water

River Eea

Grange over Sands

promenade

Cumbria

Arnside Tower

quarry

Waterslack

76   704

golf course

BARROW 15½ Miles

Allithwaite

Guides Farm

Do not attempt to cross estuary on foot
without local guidance!

'The Pepperpot'
Elmslack

Leighton Moss
R.S.P.B. reserve

B5277

Kents Bank

Kirkhead Tower

530

KENTS BANK 17½

Cumbria

Silverdale
The Shore

SILVERDALE 9¾

302

3

435

Wraysholme Tower

W.W. II aerodrome

Humphrey Head 173

Wolf House Gallery

Heald Brow 245

548   Crag Foot chimney Warton Crag

Lancashire

Jenny Brown's Point

chimney

hides

old quarry

387   340

Morecambe Bay

THE CUMBRIAN COAST line describes a wide arc around the margin of Morecambe Bay. Views from the train are dazzling, often literally so. When the sun is out and the tide in, the whole bay coruscates so vividly that you have to turn your eyes inland.

Between Carnforth and Silverdale the railway runs across a flat landscape of sheep pastures separating Warton Crag from the adjoining expanse of marsh. In the past, ill fated schemes were hatched to reclaim this land, but you have to be pretty determined to thwart the sea, and the higher 'spring' tides still regularly cover these 'ings'. Old chimneys catch the eye at Crag Foot, one either side of the line. That to seaward, near Jenny Brown's Point, was used for copper smelting. The inland chimney belonged to one of the Leighton Moss pumping houses which fell out of use during the First World War. Prior to that the valley had been reclaimed from the sea and used for agriculture since the mid 19th century. Now it has reverted to semi-wilderness, a happy course of events, for the moss is now cared for by the Royal Society for the Protection of Birds, being one of their foremost reserves, famed as a habitat for the rare Bittern and a haunt of otters as well.

The old station house at SILVERDALE has been converted into a restaurant called "Coppernobs". *Coppernob* was one of the Furness Railway Company's original locomotives, and sadly, one of only three to have survived, albeit not without a close scrape with destiny during the Second World War. Although the sea is temporarily out of sight, the railway moves picturesquely through an area of low, limestone hills on its way towards Arnside. Beyond Waterslack it crosses the boundary between Lancashire and Cumbria, formerly, here, the county of Westmorland. Deep in the woods lie the white stained rock faces of ARC's Middlebarrow Quarry, source of all the heavy lorries on the local roads.

Crossing Silverdale Moss, the woods recede briefly, and there is a glimpse to the west of Arnside Tower, one of several medieval fortifications in the area. Somewhat less fortified properties of more recent origin overlook the railway as the train slows for ARNSIDE. The station house and associated buildings have been demolished and replaced by a stone shelter, but Arnside's bare platforms still command a panoramic sweep of the Kent estuary. A lattice footbridge spans the two platforms, and from the 'up', or east side, there is access to the riverbank, along which ran the branch line to Hincaster, built in the last quarter of the 19th century for the carriage of coke from Durham to Cumbrian steelworks. There was passenger traffic too: Furness and Midland trains to Windermere, and a regular stream of invalid County Durham miners on their way to recuperate at Conishead Priory on the placid shores of Morecambe Bay. The track remained in place until 1971 to serve a quarry at Sandside, a couple of miles upstream.

Departing from Arnside the train makes the first of five esturial crossings which are such a significant feature of the Cumbrian Coast line. If the tide is in, and you are in not in a position to see the railings of the bridge, then the sensation of crossing the Kent viaduct is akin to skimming over the waves in a sea-plane. Either side, the view from the carriage window is show-stopping, be it southwards across the widening estuary with its random and constantly shifting channels, or to the north and the horizon of Lakeland summits. The viaduct itself was built to the design of James Brunlees who was later to be involved with the original 19th century Channel Tunnel scheme. At present it is being progressively rebuilt, a section at a time.

Regaining dry land, or at least the edge of the sea marsh, the line curves in a south-westerly direction towards Grange, crossing the outfall channel of the River Winster and passing the privately owned Holme Island, long since moored up to the mainland by a causeway. Grandiose Victorian hotels and nursing homes, basking in the reflected glory of their south-facing setting, herald the approach to GRANGE-OVER-SANDS, and the train pulls into a station which fulfils admirably the role of an architectural *apéritif* to this genteel resort. Cast iron canopies and sandy coloured stone buildings have welcomed holidaymakers and excursionists since the railway company decided to develop Grange as a holiday destination in the 1860s. If you want a railway parallel, Dawlish fits the bill, but Grange is more self-effacing, and miraculously seems to have avoided the slow erosion and descending spiral of standards that have spoilt other railway inspired resorts.

"The sensation of crossing the Kent viaduct is akin to skimming over the waves in a sea-plane."

During the train's brief sojourn at Grange the continuing passenger can gaze out through round-topped windows upon a seascape bounded by the west facing rim of Morecambe Bay and backed by the outline fells of the Forest of Bowland. Then, as the train departs, one can - as at Dawlish - look down on the promenade, or over ornamental gardens on the landward side of the line, and, gathering speed, absorb a blur of bandstands and boarding houses, tennis courts, cafes and a seawater swimming pool, every bit as splendid as the much better publicised route along the South Devon coastline. Approaching KENTS BANK, the train is travelling almost due south, spilling the curiously intense sunlight of this coast on to the faces of the passengers opposite you for a change. An otherwise inconspicuous house on the village side of the line is 'Guide's Farm', home of the Morecambe Bay 'sand pilots' whose work it has been, down the centuries, to guide strangers across the exposed sandbanks of the bay at low tide.

Though unstaffed now, Kents Bank station buildings remain in place, a pleasing mix of stone and timber construction. West of here the line twists inland, through a narrow, rocky cutting, away from the coastal prominence of Humphrey Head, and the rail traveller has the opportunity to catch his or her breath, as the train traverses a low lying landscape of broad fields. Wraysholme Tower is another example of a building fortified against the marauding Scots. This one, though, has been incorporated into the fabric of a working farm. During the First World War a halt was opened here to serve the adjoining rifle ranges. The grassy trackbed of a short-lived branchline can be discerned on the south side of the line. It was built to provide a link with a proposed airship factory, but the scheme was abandoned, and the railway with it. The flatlands beside the bay did become a second world war aerodrome, however, used largely for the training of pilots and gunners, but also as a base for a mountain rescue unit responding to crashes in the Lakeland fells.

Awayday to Arnside

We came up from the Midlands as a November dawn revealed frost-bitten fields. Watching Lancashire swish past the window was a comfortable prelude to a seven mile walk beside the edge of Morecambe Bay. Changing at Lancaster, the train trundled over the emptying Lune, past Hest Bank and on to the Cumbrian Coast line at Carnforth. The cold lent clarity to the landscape, and a low slung sunshine lit up the snow capped peaks of Lakeland.

Silverdale was as cold as Irkutsk. We spoke through wreaths of steam like ancient locomotives. Two elderly gentlemen were easing their trolleys out of car boots as we passed the golf course, and we thought about the old golfer late home from his round, explaining to his wife that one of them had died from a heart attack on the second hole, and that they had been slowed down by having to drag his body round the rest of the course. The road took us past Slackwood Farm where they look after injured birds of prey. A huge long-eared owl regarded us with a modicum of interest from the far side of the garden wall.

For a minor road the traffic was disconcertingly heavy, and we were glad to leave it at Crag Foot, taking to a track parallel to a channel draining Leighton Moss where there is an important RSPB reserve. We passed under the railway and crossed the dyke into a field of sheep. The pathway kept to a flood protection bank, crossing a succession of styles. We were reminded of Romney Marsh. Ducking under wind bent hawthorns bearing Furness red berries, we came to a crossing of footpaths at the foot of Heald Brow, and took the turn for Jenny Brown's Point.

We were on the marsh itself now. Skipping lithely over winding channels of water oozing out of the cropped turf. An old copper smelting chimney, which we had glimpsed from the train, stood where the marsh gave way to the shore. A road offered an easy route round to Silverdale village, but the tide was still ebbing, so we opted for the foreshore; crunching over pebbles and rocks to reach firm sand. Jenny Brown's Point crumbled into the tideline, a ruck of stones; the bay lay beyond, an infinity of sand. We skirted the rocky shore, low cliffs of limestone with trees on its tops bent like lumbago sufferers. By now the sun was warm on our backs. Oystercatchers were reflected in glassy pools abandoned by the outgoing tide; a heron flapped slowly away at our intrusive approach; across the bay a diesel train hooted its arrival at Grange-over-Sands.

Rounding Know Hill we regained *terra firma* beside a terrace of old fishermen's cottages. Shore Road led across a cattle grid into Silverdale. It was half an hour too early to obtain refreshment at the "Silverdale Hotel", so we struck across 'The Lots', a National Trust site, towards The Cove and Arnside. The sound of hammering was suggestive of alterations at Cove House, which stood masked by woods on its headland, pure Daphne du Maurier. A metalled lane led past idyllic cottages to the road. We bore left (signposted "Arnside 2") and were soon crossing from Lancashire into Cumbria. At the boundary we

Jenny Brown's Point

turned off from the road on to a footpath through a caravan site. In November the big green vans looked disconsolate, as if nostalgic for the activity of the holiday season.

On the far side of the park, the limestone lump of Arnside Knott loomed ahead through the trees and our calf muscles cried out for mercy. We bribed our brains to divert attention from the ascent, concentrating on the historic interest of Arnside Tower, a fourteenth century fortification against the threat of Scottish brigands. It overlooked an east facing valley through which the railway ran on a shallow embankment, half a mile in the distance. Cows were waiting to be milked in the farm below. We chatted to a man taking photographs. He seemed surprised that neither of us was smoking a pipe. "I could smell tobacco," he insisted, and we wondered if it was a brand favoured by the ghosts who forgather in the ruined tower.

At the top of the lane leading down to the farm, we went directly over the road and into the woods which skirt The Knott. We were back on National Trust property again, ascending a path known as "Saul's Drive". The silver birch shone like goalposts; the juniper and yew trees were as green as goalkeepers. The main track climbed steadily without appearing to head for the summit, but at intervals lesser paths broke away between the trees on our right. Unsure of the way, we chose the third of these. It quickly took us above the tree line and the views became as breath-taking as the ascent.

The summit is 521 feet above sea level, and having come from the sands themselves, we felt every foot of the climb. On the north slope

Arnside
Tower.

of the hill a toposcope outlines the peaks of Lakeland seen across the Kent estuary. Though cloud was being blown in off the sea, we could still make out the big trio of Scafell Pike, Skiddaw and Helvellyn, together with many lesser peaks closer at hand. A 'Sprinter' clattered across the Kent Viaduct and we watched while it wound its way round to Grange and Kent's Bank, wishing it had been one of the steam specials which use the route from time to time.

Suddenly the train reminded us of the timetable. "Ours is the next one," we chorused. Had we been hawks we might have soared down to the station in a trice. Being merely human, we had to scramble down the slope, and, as we descended, so did the cloud. Arnside lay like a smooth grey pebble on the edge of a muddy puddle. From the National Trust car park it was an easy lope down to the promenade, past the driveways of desirable residences with six-figure views. We picnicked on the twice rebuilt pier, closely observed by the local seagulls and pigeons, who seemed to think they had a right to a share in our sandwiches. Judging by the motley coloured feathers on some of the pigeons, it looked as though the two species were not averse to sharing spouses too.

Distance & Conditions
Start at Silverdale station, end at Arnside station. OS Landranger sheet 97. Seven miles, allow three hours net walking time. Special care needs to be taken on the foreshore between Jenny Brown's Point and Silverdale. This is best accomplished during the ebb of the tide. If the tide is coming you are recommended to detour via the road or path over the cliff top.

Refreshments
Refer to Gazetteer for details of facilities at Silverdale and Arnside.

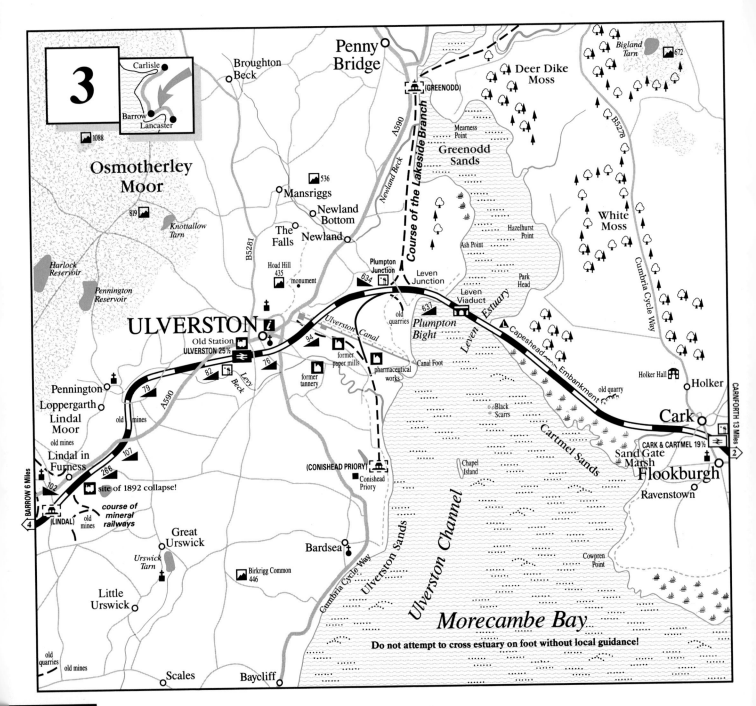

3

Carlisle

Barrow
Lancaster

▲1088

**Osmotherley
Moor**

▲819

*Knottallow
Tarn*

*Harlock
Reservoir*

*Pennington
Reservoir*

Broughton
Beck

**Penny
Bridge**

🚉 (GREENODD)

Newland Beck

Mearness
Point

**Greenodd
Sands**

*Bigland
Tarn*

▲672

**Deer Dike
Moss**

B5278

**White
Moss**

Mansriggs   ▲536

Newland
Bottom

The
Falls   Newland

B5281

Hoad Hill
435   monument

Plumpton
Junction

Leven
Junction

Ash Point

Hazelhurst
Point

Park
Head

Cumbria Cycle Way

634

637

Leven
Viaduct

old
quarries

*Plumpton
Bight*

Canal Foot

Leven Estuary

Capeshead Embankment

old quarry

Holker Hall

Holker

ULVERSTON

Old Station
ULVERSTON 25½

Ulverston Canal

94

76

former paper mills

pharmaceutical
works

former
tannery

Levy Beck

82

CARNFORTH 13 Miles

Pennington
Loppergarth
**Lindal
Moor**

old mines

**Lindal in
Furness**

79

A590

old mines

107

266

102

site of 1892 collapse!

*course of
mineral
railways*

🚉 (LINDAL)

old mines

BARROW 6 Miles   4

**Great
Urswick**

Urswick Tarn

**Little
Urswick**

old
quarries   old mines

Scales

Birkrigg Common
446

Bardsea

Cumbria Cycle Way

Ulverston Sands

Baycliff

(CONISHEAD PRIORY)

Conishead
Priory

🚉

○ Black
Scarrs

*Chapel
Island*

Ulverston Channel

Morecambe Bay

Do not attempt to cross estuary on foot without local guidance!

Cark

Cartmel Sands

CARK & CARTMEL 19½

2

**Sand Gate
Marsh**

Flookburgh

Ravenstown

*Cowpren
Point*

LIKE an elderly dowager, CARK & CARTMEL station has seen better days. But there is evidence of the graceful debutante it must once have been beneath the toll that years of neglect have taken. The 'down' side station building remains in tolerable condition, bearing a hopeful 'To Let' notice on behalf of British Rail's property department. It is typical of Ulverstone & Lancaster railway style: two storey limestone with a timber shelter. Linking the two platforms is an unusually ornate cast iron footbridge. Cark was the station for Holker Hall, and extra effort was obviously made for the resident Dukes of Devonshire. Unforgivably, the 'up' platform buildings, added later in 'Swiss chalet' style when the Furness Railway absorbed the U&L, have been demolished. Apparently the waiting room was particularly sumptuous for the benefit of the Dukes' guests. The goods shed remains in industrial use. Locally caught fish - cockles, shrimps and Flookburgh flounders - were the most significant outward traffic.

Leaving the houses of Cark and Flookburgh behind, the railway heads towards its second major estuary. Meanwhile the little River Eea seeks the sea through a muddy channel once used by small trading vessels bringing in coal and raw cotton for the local mill. One of the side benefits brought about by building the railway was the drainage and reclamation of marshland. This is amply illustrated by the Capeshead Embankment. To the south the land is still marshy and suitable only for the grazing of sheep, whilst north of the embankment the fields are fully agricultural.

Leven viaduct repeats the excitement of the Kent crossing. It is an even longer structure and subject to a 30mph speed restriction. So there is a moment or two to savour the views: northwards towards the heights of Grizedale Forest; southwards over Cartmel Sands and the Ulverston Channel. Like a children's game of objects on a tray, you try to remember as much of what you have seen as you can: the monument on Hoad Hill, Chapel Island, Conishead Priory and, far across the bay, the shoebox like outline of Heysham's nuclear power stations. Winds have a tendency to funnel up the estuary. In February, 1903 the rolling stock of the Carnforth to Whitehaven mail was blown over, but not off the viaduct, and its passengers had to crawl to safety through the wind and darkness. Subsequently a wind speed recorder was placed at the western end of the viaduct and connected to alarm bells in the signal boxes at Plumpton, Ravensbarrow and Cark. Its modern equivalent can be seen on the seaward side at the Cark end. If the wind exceeds seventy miles an hour an alarm rings in the signal box at Plumpton Junction and services are suspended until the wind subsides.

A classic Furness Railway signal box, dating from 1897, superintends the track layout at Plumpton Junction. You catch a glimpse of potted plants in the window and, possibly, a short train of chemical wagons destined for the Glaxo Works in the exchange siding. For all this, though, Plumpton box enjoys just a distant echo of its former importance, in the days when it controlled the east and west curves on to the Lakeside branch, the Conishead Priory branch, the arrival and departure of banking engines engaged on the climb to Lindal, and access to the local quarry sidings. Passenger services on the Lakeside branch were withdrawn in 1965, four years short of the line's centenary. In its heyday it had been an immensely popular tourist link with Lake Windermere upon which the Furness Railway provided its own steamer service to Bowness and Ambleside. The top 3½ miles of the branch

have been preserved and are operated as a steam line by the Lakeside & Haverthwaite Railway, whose summer services still connect with the lake's steamers.

The train approaches ULVERSTON at rooftop level under the watchful gaze of the Sir John Barrow monument on Hoad Hill, crosses the town's eponymous canal, and comes to a halt in one of the most magnificent small town stations in England. Given the reasonable frequency of trains on this part of the Cumbrian Coast line, it is difficult, and unnecessary, to resist the urge to alight and enjoy the details of Paley & Austin's Italianate architecture. Dating from 1874, it was actually the *third* station provided for the town. The original terminus of the line from Barrow stands alongside at a higher level. Not exactly lacking in architectural merit itself, this station - senior by twenty years to Messrs P & A's - is now used occasionally as a car showroom. Deliveries of fuel oil from the refineries at Stanlow are made by train to the sidings at the rear of the old station during the winter months. When the railway was extended eastwards, an interim set of through platforms was provided to the east of the present station, but the Furness company, like many independent lines of the period, had an inordinate pride in their railway and sought to make a lasting architectural statement reflecting the solidity and stature of its undertaking.

Having clung, limpet like, to the coast since Carnforth, and in doing so avoided any noticeably adverse gradients, beyond Ulverston the Furness Railway has a profile like the side of a roof. Climbing the best part of 250 feet in three miles, westbound trains have their work cut out, even in these dieselised days, to reach the summit at Lindal. During one of its financially more successful periods, the Furness Railway proposed a gradient free coastwise link between Ulverston and Barrow, extending the Conishead branch southwards along the coast past Bardsea and Baycliff. But before any work could be done, the region experienced one of its periodical economic depressions, and the plans were shelved. In terms of distance the scheme wouldn't have made much difference, but elsewhere this much indented coastline, with its wide estuaries, creates several curious anomalies in mileage. From Cark to Ulverston, for example, it's a dozen roundabout miles by road, but under half that by rail across the Leven viaduct. On the other hand, as the crow flies, Ulverston to Millom is just seven miles, yet a staggering twenty-six by train via the Barrow loop.

But back on the Barrow bound train, the underfloor diesel motors are reving hard and the wheels beating out a slow, rhythmic clickety-clack as the line ascends past Pennington to Lindal. Deep cuttings, some with steep sloping banks of wild vegetation, others hewn vertically out of the rock, temporarily mask the surrounding countryside which, when the summit is reached, is revealed as a quasi moorland scene of scattered farms interspersed with the telltale scar tissue of old iron mines and mineral railways, like a farmer who has been in a fight. Lindal's claim to railway fame - or should it be immortality - is that on 22nd September, 1892 a sudden outbreak of subsidence caused a deep hole to appear in the path of an approaching goods train. The engine, but not the tender, vanished into the yawning cavity, never to reappear. It is still down there, somewhere, a railway age treasure trove. Lindal Tunnel was originally dug to take a single track. It was later doubled by the simple expediency of cutting a larger outer tunnel then demolishing the original inner lining.

An Inland Lighthouse

The little orange 'Pacer' limped along the coast line. Since Silverdale it had been having alterations with the gears on which these bus like vehicles depend. Luckily there were no adverse gradients before Ulverston or our walk might have had to have been aborted. At Arnside a plate-layer had got on surreptitiously with a bulge in his day-glo vest. Two spindly legs dangled revealingly from its hem. One of the perks of the job. Beyond the Leven Viaduct came appetising glimpses of the walk ahead: the signal box at Plumpton Junction; the lighthouse like monument on Hoad Hill; and the old Ulverston Canal reflecting the deep blue sky that this winter morning had gone out of its way to provide.

Whether or not the train made Barrow, what with all those climbs in the vicinity of Lindal, we never got to know, but it decanted us amidst the palatial surroundings of Ulverston station more or less on schedule and we set off into the town. Bathed in the diffuse golden glow of a brittle November sun, Ulverston looked immediately attractive, but we had a little matter of seven miles to walk before getting to know the place better.

Pausing only to gather some leaflets from the Tourist Information Centre, we followed County Road, the A590, in a north-easterly direction out of town. Feelings of sadness assailed us as we passed Hartley's doomed brewery. Its owners, Robinsons, the Stockport brewers, had decided to close it down after 288 years in existence. The "Canal Tavern", at which point our walk really began, was still advertising the local 'beer from the wood' at under a pound a pint, but we wondered how much more it would start to cost after being brought in by road from Cheshire.

The Ulverston Canal's heyday was a brief one, the railway saw it off in the cynical way that most railways treated most canals, but at the turn of the 18th century four or five hundred ships a year were sailing up the 1½ mile canal to berth on Ulverston's doorstep. Its placid waters are now the resort of anglers and its towing path a metalled road belonging to the nearby pharmaceutical factory. The public, though, have a right of way and we found it pleasant going, passing, at intervals, old stone warehouses reiterating the waterway's erstwhile commercial importance. We tried to picture sloops and barquentines moored at the wharves, but a tractor towing a pungent trailer of manure broke into our historic reverie.

Two railways cross the canal: the Cumbrian Coast line itself, and, less obviously, a single track branch made up of somewhat rusty rails, which serves the Glaxochem plant. It looked to us as though the line had fallen out of use, but there were wagons in the sidings on the far bank. Frequent tannoy announcements rang round the works, machinery hummed, and plumes of white vapour issued from glistening metal chimneys into the still air. Two thousand people are employed here in the 'round the clock' manufacture of antibiotics.

Gradually we began to make out the canal's seaward end and the old entrance lock into the Leven estuary. The lock was sealed off

Canal head, Ulverston.

during the Second World War; perhaps the authorities had got wind of a German plan to sail up the canal and capture Ulverston. The tide was on the ebb. A fisherman had two rods propped up on the pier. The view was intoxicating. Chapel Island stood silhouetted to the south-east. Heysham power station was a pale rectangle on the horizon. There was that sort of end of the world feel about the place peculiar to coastal hamlets.

A road led northwards along the shore of Plumpton Bight. Passing between some houses, it became an easily followed grassy path overlooking the canal and the pharmaceutical works. Skirting an old quarry, Hoad Hill, the intended climax of our walk, came enticingly into view, its brackeny ramparts glowing a russety colour in the bright sunshine. The path led obviously enough across a series of small pastures. A railway signal gleamed white ahead as we approached Plumpton Junction. Two magpies regarded us quizically from the edge of a wood fringing old quarry workings. Smoke curled up from the redbrick signal cabin and, as if on cue, a light blue coloured shunter came cautiously off the branch to refute our fears that the line had closed. In its wake it brought a quintet of tank wagons to be deposited in the exchange siding.

Having watched the shunting engine perform its ancient rites, we crossed the railway by way of the lane leading to Plumpton Hall and headed for Newland. A few yards later on we crossed the flooded trackbed of the old branch to Lakeside on Windermere. The lane wound picturesquely onward, past a field of lowing cattle. A wren fidgeted in the hedgerow and, in the corner of another field, an old railway box van did service as a hay store.

A dog barked indignantly as we crossed Newland Beck, flowing almost due north to meet the Leven at Greenodd, blissfully unaware that it would have to flow all the way back again once it had joined the bigger watercourse. Shimmying rapidly between roaring cars, we left the main road and made for Newland Bottom. The barking dog still hadn't got us out of his system, but we were oblivious, intent instead on the chatter of the beck, bounding over its bed on our left. The map labelled the hills on our right as 'The Alps', and there was certainly an Alpine brevity and abruptness about the neigbouring pastures, even if the cattle weren't wearing bells.

Woodsmoke filled the still air at Newland Bottom, a spattering of houses tucked reclusively in a deep fold beside the beck. One of them looked as though it might once have been a mill of some sort. It was here that we inadvertently misread the map. We *thought* that two footpaths splayed outwards on the far side of the bridge spanning the beck, and it seemed to us that the left hand one of these would take us more or less directly to the top of Hoad Hill. We *were* surprised that there was no signpost on the bridge, but regular ramblers will know that such absences mean nothing. Passing through a metal gate, the way seemed clear at first, up a rocky track through a wood. But it soon became apparent that we heading south-east, rather than due south, so we struck across the field we were in, passing directly through one dilapidated drystone wall, and being glad to discover a style across the next one. It was not until we were speeding home on the train that the penny dropped. Closer inspection of the map revealed that there *isn't* a direct right of way from Newland Bottom to Hoad Hill. Officially, we should have gone the long way round by way of 'The Falls'. So if you plan to follow in our footsteps, make sure you do the right thing!

Meanwhile, blissfully ignorant of our small trespass, we toiled up the north facing slopes of Hoad Hill, making full use of a 'kissing gate', and, as we breasted the summit, being rewarded by the most extravagant of panoramas. Turning slowly through 360 degrees, we took in the snow-capped heights of Lakeland, the mirror like surface of the Leven estuary, Morecambe Bay backed by the Trough of Bowland, and out beyond all this to the west, the glistening expanse of the Irish Sea. Casting our back-packs on the springy turf, we drank in this vista, attempting to retain its images like students cramming for an examination. Above us rooks made raucous mirth, below the chimney pots of Ulverston fumed vertically. The whole walk lay visible below us and we mentally retraced our steps: down the towpath beside the canal; along the shore; through the fields to Plumpton Junction, where the wagons were still waiting to be collected by a main line engine; and up the country lane to Newland.

Plumpton Junction.

Nearby, the Barrow Monument stood its ground, having dominated the Ulverston skyline since its erection in 1850. It commemorates Sir John Barrow, a local lad made good, who explored much of the world before becoming Secretary to the Admiralty, hence the nautical theme apparent in the design of the structure. Even on a winter weekday, there were plenty of people on the hilltop; two lads on mountain bikes; a man equipped with a back-pack so heavy he might have been on a much longer walk than ours; solitary figures with dogs; and a lady with a sketch-pad. Visually replete, we essayed a helter-skelterish descent, passing seats commemorating others who had valued the same ravishing view.

Distance & Conditions
Start and finish at Ulverston station. OS Landranger sheets 96 or 97. Seven miles, allow three hours. No problems with conditions underfoot.

Refreshments
Refer to Gazetteer for details of Ulverston.

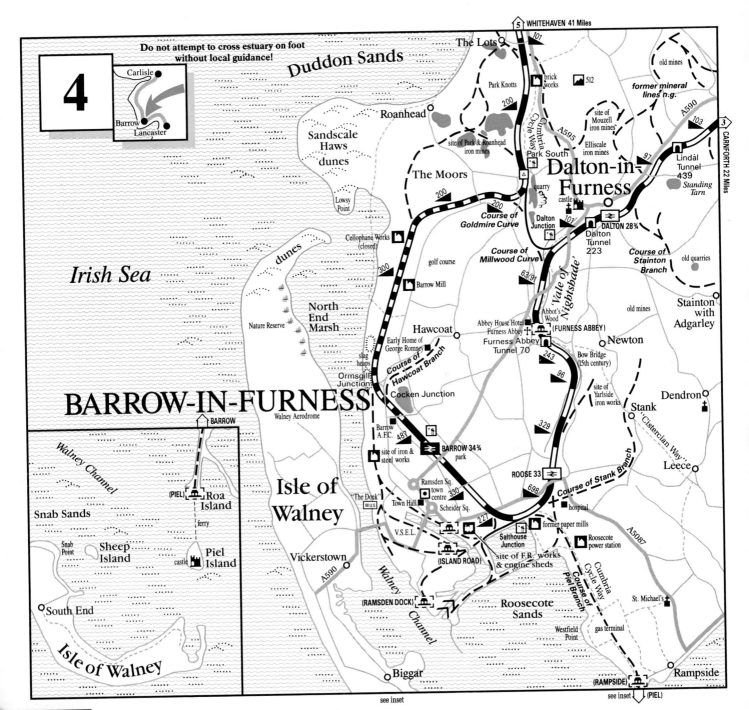

4

see inset

THE TRAIN drops down into DALTON like a ball bearing on a pin table: wheel on rail; steel to steel; mirror bright. Waiting on Dalton platform, it can be heard roaring along the embankments, ricocheting through the cuttings and braking, eventually to pause alongside - with deference to the present domestic inhabitants - the fairly sombre station building, a lugubriously grey structure of local slate. Shorn of its canopies and other appurtenances, the station has come down in the world with a bump. Empty beer cans lie scattered in the lean-to waiting room whose walls are liberally devoted to local graffiti. Through murky window panes one can spy across the station yard upon the comings and goings of the prefabricated police station. British Rail have opted out of responsibility for stations such as this. Shouldn't, then, the local populace rise up and take a communal pride in their reception counter with the outside world?

When this first stretch of the Furness Railway opened in 1846, catering for passengers was an afterthought; ore was the business in hand! Human freight was conveyed only on Sundays, apparently in a converted cattle wagon. New to the job, the young James Ramsden, who quickly worked his way to prominence within the company, discovered the line's sole driver the worse for drink, and took over the controls himself for the next few days until a replacement could be sent up from the Liverpool & Manchester Railway. Deep in these thoughts, one barely notices departure from Dalton, passage through a short tunnel, and the advent of Dalton Junction, curving away from which, goes the Barrow avoiding loop, rounding a tall embankment masked by tawny trees. To the west the former Millwood curve can be discerned, having been abandoned just before the turn of the century. Along with the line from Lindal and Dalton that we have travelled down, this had been the earliest part of the Furness Railway, linking Barrow harbour with slate quarries in the vicinity of Kirkby.

Now begins an unexpectedly beautiful interlude, as the railway threads sinuously through the Vale of Nightshade and past the gracious purlieus of Furness Abbey. Even in ruins, the abbey creates a noble impression. Surpassed in importance only by Fountains Abbey in Yorkshire, the Cistercian order here possessed most of the Furness peninsula as well as holding lands on the Isle of Man and in Ireland too. The abbey thrived for four centuries but was stripped of its roof and half-heartedly demolished after the Dissolution in 1537. Three hundred years later, the Furness Railway set about building a line through its grounds, drawing poetic wrath from William Wordsworth, who branded the company "profane despoilers", whilst empathising with the "grave demeanour" of the navvies going about their work in what he supposed was awe of the religious splendour surrounding them. In Wordsworth's eyes, railways were anathema. Two years earlier he had penned a sonnet against the building of the Kendal & Windermere line. But what chance have poets against Progress? Could Betjeman or Larkin have stopped a motorway from being built?

From the outset the Furness Railway realised the tourist potential presented by the romantically ruined abbey. Early excursionists voyaged by steamer from Fleetwood to Piel Pier, going on by train to a station opened in the abbey grounds. The Manor House was enlarged into a sumptuous hotel with a covered approach from the station. Advertised as being located in the *centre* of Lakeland, and boasting a ballroom with a sprung dance floor, it was promoted as "the favourite resort of the Artist, Antiquary and Lover of the Picturesque". King George V and Queen Mary stopped off at the hotel in 1917 on their way to visit the Barrow shipyards. Under L.M.S. auspices, however, the establishment declined and closed in 1938. During the war it was used as an anti-aircraft control base, until badly hit in the air raid of 1941. Subsequently it was demolished, though a portion survives as the "Abbey Tavern". The station, too, has vanished, following closure in 1950; a great shame for modern day pilgrims to the ruins. Now what would Wordsworth have made of the car park? Others were attracted to the bosky charms of the Vale of Nightshade. James Ramsden made a large enough fortune out of the railway to build a mansion called Abbot's Wood on land to the east of the line. His private saloon was stabled overnight in a special siding to facilitate speedy access to the office in Barrow each morning. On the opposite side of the valley, the directors of Vickers shipyard brought in no lesser an architect than Edwin Lutyens to design The Abbey House in 1913, though it has been described by experts as one of his 'gloomiest' buildings. Nowadays it survives as a hotel, but Ramsden's old place has been demolished and school parties giggle their way along the nature trail through his woodlands.

"Now begins an unexpectedly beautiful interlude, as the railway threads sinuously through the Vale of Nightshade and past the gracious purlieus of Furness Abbey."

Curving under gorse covered hills, once extensively mined, the line reaches ROOSE (some rhyme it with mousse, as in chocolate, others with screws, as in GKN) a brutally minimalist station overlooked by bay-windowed semi-detached villas, with decorative gables. Into a landscape of redbrick terraced streets, horizoned by mammoth dockyard cranes and the vaguely Flemish tower of the town hall, the railway enters the suburbs of the town it spawned. Old maps depict a melee of branchlines and sidings issuing in every conceivable direction from Salthouse Junction. Present reality is a rusty single track twisting towards the quay where ships berth with nuclear waste destined for the Sellafield complex up the coast. Vanished are the lines which enmeshed each dock, penetrated the gargantuan haematite works, and fanned out into phalanxes of goods yards, carriage sidings, engine sheds and railway engineering works.

One branch led across the moveable Buccleuch Bridge to Ramsden Dock station from whence steamers plied to Fleetwood, Douglas and Belfast until the outbreak of the First World War. Operation of the Belfast route was shared with the Midland Railway, but Barrow was too remote a port of embarkation for most mainlanders, though the eight hour voyage competed favourably with other transit times. More successful, was the Furness Railway's steamer service between Fleetwood and Barrow. The company promoted a circular tour for holidaymakers at Blackpool from where they were conveyed to Fleetwood dock by tram. An hour's voyage to Barrow by steamer was followed by an excursion by special train to Lake Side, Windermere for lunch. In the afternoon the itinerary included a trip by steam yacht to Ambleside and a charabanc ride to Coniston, returning by train to Ramsden Dock for a 7pm sailing back to Fleetwood. The fare for this 100 mile round trip was 8 shillings third class and 12 shillings in the luxury of first; slightly less, in other words, than the price of an Intercity cup of tea today.

By the end of the 19th century, the Furness Railway had spent over two million pounds developing Barrow docks, leaving them third in size only to London and Liverpool, but the directors' ambition to create a trans-Atlantic port was never realised. Nevertheless, the density of the railway network caused considerable operating difficulties, and a new central station was opened in 1882. It is at this station that our train arrives today, though it would be unrecognisable to passengers accustomed to using it before the Second World War, for in May 1941 it was extensively damaged by enemy bombers. Architecturally the station was typical of the Furness Railway's flamboyant approach; a huge barn of place with a timber clad overall roof which might have looked more at home gracing some remote junction in an obscure corner of the Austro-Hungarian empire. Sadly it was blown to smithereens, including a splendidly ornate gazebo which housed an ancient Furness locomotive nicknamed *Coppernob*. The engine survived the experience and now resides in the National Railway Museum at York.

The post war replacement of BARROW station has its own ersatz charm. The concourse incorporates the Furness Railway's memorial to its employees killed in the First World War; a little knocked about by shrapnel, but all the more moving for that. A frontier feel pervades the station, only a few services run through from North to South or vice versa. In the mid-Eighties Barrow lost its through Intercity link with London. Presumably there were no longer enough submarine salesmen journeying to the embassies and consulates of the capital to merit the direct service.

So rationalisation has taken its toll, but at least the Cumbrian Coast route remains intact and under no forseeable threat. So relax in the comfortably upholstered saloon of the Class 153 diesel unit and watch from the window as the train attempts to extricate itself from the industrial clutches of Barrow's northern outskirts. Barrow Association Football Club suffered the ignominy of having to seek re-election to the Fourth Division on six occasions before finally being put out of its misery in 1973. In 1992 the club sank further still, being relegated from the GM Vauxhall Conference league. The ground seems to shoulder charge the railway as the train creeps slowly past acres of empty carriage sidings, but there is no 'yellow card'. The old junctions of Cocken and Ormsgill are just memories now, as is another Furness Railway tourist initiative, the purchase of 18th century portrait painter George Romney's childhood home at High Cocken, and its opening as a public attraction. The admission charge of one penny was waived for holders of rail or steamer tickets, and a refreshment pavilion was erected in the grounds.

The line becomes single track, worked by 'tokenless block', curving under mountainous slag heaps which eventually subside to reveal the northern tip of the Isle of Walney, an expanse of dunes and shingle occupied, amongst other flora and fauna by the rare natterjack toad. Both ends of Walney are classified Sites of special Scientific Interest, as are the National Trust's Sandscale Haws, another semi-wild landscape of marram grass and wind blown sand hills also visible from the train as it twists and turns towards the junction at Park South. Remember Dalton, nine miles back along the Barrow loop? Here it's just a mile away on foot!

The curve connecting Oaklea and Goldmire junctions closed in 1908, but its course is still easily detected. The attractively designed Park South signal box is a twin of that at St Bees. For a comparatively small company, the Furness Railway took considerable trouble with the architecture of their buildings. Their trains were also pleasing to the eye: 'indian' red locomotives and blue and white carriages. Hamilton Ellis wrote that "A Furness train looked at its best in strong evening sunshine between showers, with the rainy Cumbrian hills all around."

Due North heads the train for Askam, negotiating a landscape that has undergone great change. In 1851 huge deposits of iron ore were discovered here. Antiquarian maps reveal the extent of the pits which were either prosaically numbered or sentimentally named: Betty Pit, Rita Pit, Peggy Pit, Kathleen Pit and so on. In their heyday over twenty pits were producing half a million tons of ore per annum, but that prosperity was relatively shortlived, and many of the pits were finally abandoned during the Depression of the 1930s. Now the workings are covered by a huge landfill site across which huge earthmovers drag themselves like mechanical dinosaurs. Some parts of the site have been flooded and are now a haven for wildfowl; and there's even a trout farm. In the midst of all this, Park Farm, once beseiged by mineral lines and quarry faces, keeps a herd of deer on the rolling, fenced pastures of The Knotts. The Askam Brickworks of the Furness Brick & Tile Co. dates back to the middle of the 19th century. Until the Sixties a narrow gauge tramway linked the works with a shale pit to the rear of Park Farm.

Island Hopping Furness Style

There are five islands off Barrow. The largest is Walney, the smallest is Sheep. We planned an itinerary setting foot on three of them - Roa, Piel and Walney - and offering close up views of Foulney and Sheep. For once in our travels the *tide*tables were more important than the *time*tables. Our first island, Roa, is attached to the mainland by a causeway, but from there to Piel it is necessary to employ the services of a ferryman, and his trade is dependent on the tide. From Piel to Walney we intended to walk across the sands, impassable for certain periods either side of high water. So we plotted and we planned for a day when the tides and the trains were propitious, and on a Thursday in May, when high water was 8.7 metres at Ramsden Dock, we caught the train to Roose to begin a day of island hopping, Furness style.

It was the first heat wave of the year. We walked down tree-lined Roose Road, turned left after half a mile into Salthouse Road, then left again at "The Sandgate" pub along a metalled, but potholed road (signposted "Cumbria Coastal Way") which passed beneath the railway. Beyond the railway the path rose up to the lip of Cavendish Dock and we were immediately in a different world. An onshore breeze brought a salty tang with it and to the west, across the sheet of water, stood the skyline of Barrow backed by the outline of Black Combe.

Cavendish Dock acts as a reservoir of cooling water for Roosecote power station. Beyond it lie the open waters of Roosecote Sands. It was twenty past ten, exactly high water according to the tidetable. Saltwater lapped against a fringe of marsh beside the raised bank on which we were walking. Oystercatchers stood at the waters edge, and a distant, white sailed yacht made its way down Walney Channel to the open sea. Once upon a time this raised bank had been a railway linking Barrow to Roa Island. Built to carry ore to a deep water pier, it had enjoyed a Victorian and Edwardian heyday of day-trippers. A century ago we could have crowded in with the crinolined, blazered and flanneled throng trundling down to the islands by steam. Now a gas works blocks the railbed, and the path is diverted around Westfield Point where the gorse smells like melted butter and you catch your first view of the island of Piel.

A car windscreen glinted from the causeway to Roa. The breeze stiffened but it was still hot. The path curved inland to rejoin the old railway. Sheep grazed in the neighbouring fields, larks and lapwings soared overhead. Delighted, like us, with the day, sedge warblers and reed buntings improvised melodies in the hedgerows. Past static caravans we came to Rampside, where the old station platform is a still discernible bank in the undergrowth. A house called "Station Bungalow" used to be the ticket office. Immediately beyond it we

moved out on to the causeway to Roa which had borne rails until the line closed in 1936. A third of the way down the causeway a track struck out to the left towards Foulney Island. At this state of the tide it was vitually covered; certainly impassable to vehicles, possible, though foolhardy perhaps, to reach on foot.

Sea thrift flowered amidst the dandelions and daisies on the grassy verge of the causeway. It had been built by a London banker in the 1840s with an eye to making a fortune in tolls from the passage of both passengers and goods along the causeway to the deep water pier on Roa Island. He wanted, he said, to link Roa Island "with the neighbouring island of Great Britain!" A couple of windsurfers were making the most of the easterly breeze which was rattling the halyards of the yachts at the Roa Island Boating Club. Even though it has its umbilical cord to the mainland, Roa has the feel of an island about it. Schneider, the Barrow steel magnate, built a summer residence here and called it "Villa Marina" and terraced cottages were provided for the pilotmen of Barrow harbour.

Roa slumbered in the noonday heat and we made our assignation with Mr Diamond, one of three ferrymen currently employed on the somewhat whimsical and seasonal trade in passengers to Piel Island. We came upon him in the back yard of his former pilots house. "You're early," he said "I haven't got the boat ready yet!" He was a tall, quietly spoken man in his late sixties; possibly older but physically very fit. He had the conversational knack of transforming an inquiry into an instruction. "Perhaps you could come out in the small boat to get the ferry with me?" We took this as a compliment and followed him down to the slipway where his 'small' boat was waiting to be rolled into the water. "It's going to be difficult," said Mr Diamond "it's an easterly

Piel Island.

wind, we might not get off; and even if we do, we might not find it easy landing on Piel." Mr Diamond was, we began to appreciate, a man inclined to cross his bridges before he came to them."

We took off our socks and our shoes and helped Mr Diamond to push the boat out across the shingle and into deeper water. He got aboard and we passed him the oars, then a wave picked up the boat and put it back on the beach. We became quite adept at pushing the boat out, but the waves and the wind were equal to our efforts. "Perhaps you could get in the boat and we could push off with the oars?" instructed Mr Diamond. This idea worked tolerably well, though we became rather wetter than we'd bargained for in the process.

The ferry lay a couple of hundred yards offshore and it needed all Mr Diamond's inheritance of seaman's vigour and cunning to get us to it. It was called *Boy David* and Mr Diamond had acquired it from a fisherman in Poole, at which port it was still officially registered. We clambered aboard and attached the tender's 'painter' to the ferry, taking in the scenic details of the surrounding foreshore while the ferryman attended to the engine. "Perhaps I'll land you on the other side of the island?", expressed Mr Diamond "that easterly will make it very difficult at the jetty." His tone lent a certain *gravitas* to the proceedings. We began to appreciate that it would be touch and go whether we reached Piel more or less intact or whether our bodies would be subsequently washed ashore.

The ferry moved imperceptibly towards the island, imperceptibly, that is, on a horizontal plane; vertically things were all too perceptible as we lurched from wave to wave. "It isn't usually so choppy," intoned Mr Diamond, tacitly ignoring the deepening emerald hue of our complexions. Soon, though, we were to leeward of Piel, the sea calmed down and Mr Diamond was wondering if it would be possible to test the depth of water with his boat hook. He also wondered if it would be possible for us to get hold of his mooring buoy. "I keep it here for emergencies," he added with pride. The manoeuvre went surprisingly well. *Boy David* was attached to the buoy and we were rowed ashore in the tender, wading the last few yards and waving to the admirable Mr D, as we made our first real landfall of the day.

If it was off the coast of Devon, Piel Island would be bogged down with tourists. It has all the ingredients to be a honeypot: a romantically ruined 14th century castle, a convival inn, and plenty of that indefinable magic that small islands hold for our island race. But because it is on the doorstep of Barrow, Piel remains remote and unvisited, save for the occasional hot summer weekend when trade is brisk enough to occupy the waking hours of the three authorised ferrymen of Roa. Even on this warm weekday we were the only people booked on the ferry and, though noon had come and gone, the door of the "Ship Inn" was resolutely locked. No matter, the castle was ours for the taking, and we captured it splendidly; storming the gateway, marauding on the battlements and indulging our own delicious fantasies and adventures.

We sat out of the wind at the top of one of the towers and watched the ebb tide gradually revealing an expanse of sand, across which we planned to walk to the next island on our itinerary, Walney. When we came down from our redoubt the pub had miraculously opened and a hubbub of voices issued from the shadowy confines of its cool bar. Four or five fishermen were paying court to the 'King of Piel', otherwise known as the landlord of the "Ship Inn". Mr Diamond had told us it would be safe to set out for Walney three hours after high

water but we thought a little local knowledge wouldn't go amiss. "Three hours!" came the fisherman's chorus, like something out of "The Pirates of Penzance". "Did Tony tell you that?" We sheepishly acknowledged that it had indeed been Mr T. Diamond's advice. "Jesus could do it," said one of them looking us up and down "but you couldn't." "More like four hours," said another. The landlord led us out towards the jetty. "See that piece of seaweed?" he asked, "when you can see the whole of a rock beneath us, then you can set off for Walney." So we bought some beer and kept an eye on the seaweed and, to be fair to all parties, the rock stood fully revealed after three and a half hours, so we bade farewell to the assembly and set off on the next leg of our journey.

We marched past the row of pilots cottages ("1875 - Honi Soit Que Maly Pense") and out on to the glistening sands, warm and wet beneath our feet. The landlord had told us to follow his marker stakes: "We've got reflectors on them for night work," he had added mysteriously. They were easily followed, though once or twice we had to ford deeper pools left by the tide. On our left lay Sheep Island, though judging by its inhabitants it might have better been known as Gull Island. At the turn of the century the harbour commissioners of Barrow erected an isolation hospital on it to deal with infectious seamen, but now the island was totally deserted, save for the gulls who, it's said, don't take kindly to human visitors; especially at nesting time.

As we neared Walney the sand turned to mud and we could hear the water draining out of it. Walney exuded a mainland air. Cars roared past on the road and what we took to be a gull colony turned out to be a landfill site. It was warm going and we looked back fondly on Piel, already nostalgic for its isolation and cooling breeze. In another context the pasturelands of South Walney might have had their own charm, but our itinerary was coming to a close with an inescapable sense of anti-climax. The dust carts of Barrow bore down on us and it seemed a long way to the bus stops of Vickerstown. Beyond the village of Biggar we drew level with the dockyards of Barrow. High and dry at low tide they seemed strangely surreal, as if the ships at berth had got there by more devious means than navigation. We caught a No.1 into town and were treated to a tour of Vickerstown's housing estates, bustling with home-going mothers and their infants. Then we dipped down over the Walney Channel, a trickle of water bounded by shelving banks of shining mud, and passed the huge submarine and engineering works. Our island hopping was over, and we had reached the largest of them all - it was called England.

Distance & Conditions
Start from Roose station, finish at Barrow. OS Landranger Sheet 96. Nine miles walking plus ferry and bus. Allow up to eight hours depending on the tides. No problems with walking but it is essential to pre-book the ferry. Tony Diamond's telephone number is Barrow (0229) 821741. Other ferrymen are contactable on 820983 and 820941. Make sure, as well, that you pay attention to local advice regarding crossing the sands between Piel and Walney. To lessen the amount of walking you could catch a bus from central Barrow to Roa Island but these don't run on Sundays. Tel: Barrow 821325 for timetable details.

Refreshments
There are suburban shops between Roose station and Salthouse where the basis of a picnic can be obtained. On Roa Island there's a pub and a cafe ("The Bosun's Locker"). On Piel there's the "Ship Inn", and at Biggar - on Walney - "The Queen's Arms".

SHAPED like a croquet hoop, the railway negotiates its third estuary. Kent, Leven, and now Duddon, another watercourse sprung from the high Lakeland fells, in this case the Wrynose Pass. There were 19th century proposals to bridge the estuary between Askam and Millom, and materials were stockpiled on the banks of the Duddon, but the railway company drew back from the expense of actually constructing the viaduct, and so today's commuters between Millom and Barrow (of which there are plenty because the road journey is even more dilatory) have an extra three quarters of an hour or so eaten out of their lives each day. Their frustration is the tourist's gain, as the train follows one bank and then the other of the sandy estuary. If the crossing had been made lower down, the land upstream of the embankment would have been reclaimed for agricultural use, and this tidal, seabird haunted wilderness would have been lost for ever.

But we are running ahead of ourselves, and must first consider the architectural merit of ASKAM station, another of Paley & Austin's little gems. On this occasion the dominant feature is the deep expanse of tiled roof on the platform side of the building, an ingenious alternative to a cast iron canopy. The practice's usual imaginative mix of timber and masonry embellishments adds further character to an already striking building. Look, for instance, at the north end where the gentlemen's toilet rounds off the building with an architectural fanfare. For all its latent beauty, though, the station desperately needs a new purpose in life if it is not to decay to the point at which demolition becomes the only feasible option.

North of Askam the broad estuary of the Duddon comes into view. Two miles away the steeple of Millom church beckons, but there are still ten railway miles to go until we reach the former iron-making town, whose rooftops merge into a horizon bounded by the high bulk of Black Combe, looking like something out of a Japanese print. Meanwhile, back on the east bank of the Duddon, a golfing links stretches up from Askam's outskirts until its way is barred by the limestone outcrop of Dunnerholme, which looks as though it belongs to some other, quite different, landscape. Millions of years ago it may

have been a coral reef bathed by much warmer waters.

Now the railway, paralleled closely by the new "Cumbria Coastal Way", effects another scene change, moving into marshland, the predominate, but by no means the only, landscape for the rest of the journey round the estuary's ill defined edge to Millom. Such sudden topographical changes leave you spinning. Look eastwards from the train and you would think you were in the Yorkshire Dales as the eye travels up to the heathery tops of Bank House Moor. Look west, and were it not for the fells rearing up beyond the far margin of the river, the foreground might be Norfolk.

"A horizon bounded by the high bulk of Black Combe, looking like something out of a Japanese print."

KIRKBY-IN-FURNESS was said to boast the 'longest station seat in the world'. Now it doesn't have a station seat at all. But the demolition of the booking hall and sundry other station buildings, can't detract from the attractive setting overlooking a winding creek called Kirkby Pool. As the line swings north-west it is just possible to discern the original course of the Furness Railway to its 1846 terminus at the slate wharf at Wall End, from whence it was linked by a still prominent inclined plane to the Burlington slate quarries high up on the escarpment of Kirkby Moor. Slate is still being cut up there, but, inevitably, it all goes out by lorry along the A5092 now. Kirkby Pool flows down from the fells overlooking Coniston Water. Crossing it where it widens lazily to meet the Duddon, the railway passes Angerton Hall, an isolated farm, sheltered from the estuary's winds by a mask of trees. Then marsh gives way to moss, a wilderness of peat, its dark soil accentuating the silvery bark of the birch trees which always thrive in such surroundings.

In the good old days FOXFIELD was where you changed trains for the journey up the breath-takingly pretty branch line to Coniston. For this service (and that of the Lakeside Branch) the Furness Railway workshops at Barrow turned out a pair of 'railmotor cars' (that is,

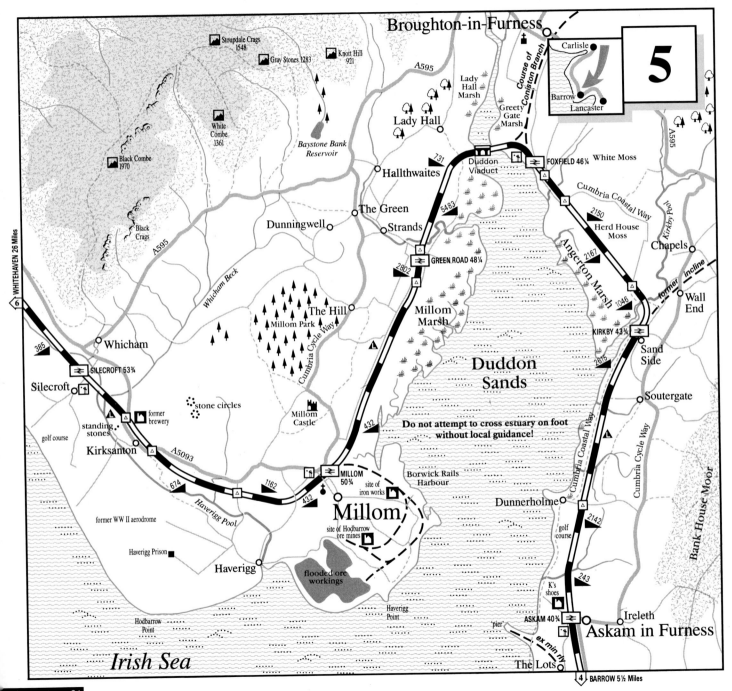

Broughton-in-Furness

5

Carlisle
Barrow
Lancaster

Stoupdale Crags 1548
Gray Stones 1283
Knott Hill 921

A595

Lady Hall Marsh
Greety Gate Marsh
Course of Coniston Branch

White Combe 1361
Baystone Bank Reservoir

Lady Hall

Black Combe 1970

Hallthwaites

731

Duddon Viaduct

FOXFIELD 46¼
White Moss

Cumbria Coastal Way

WHITEHAVEN 26 Miles

6

The Green

Dunningwell

Strands

5483

2150

Herd House Moss

Chapels

Black Crags

385

A595

Whicham Beck

GREEN ROAD 48¼

2802

Millom Marsh

Angerton Marsh

2167

former incline

Wall End

1046

The Hill

Millom Park

Cumbria Cycle Way

Whicham

SILECROFT 53¾

Silecroft

stone circles

Millom Castle

432

Duddon Sands

KIRKBY 43¾

2815

Sand Side

Soutergate

standing stones

former brewery

golf course

Kirksanton

A5093

674

1162

432

MILLOM 50¾

Millom

site of iron works

Do not attempt to cross estuary on foot without local guidance!

Borwick Rails Harbour

Dunnerholme

Cumbria Coastal Way

Cumbria Cycle Way

Bank House Moor

former WW II aerodrome

Haverigg Pool

site of Hodbarrow ore mines

golf course

2142

Haverigg Prison

Haverigg

flooded ore workings

Haverigg Point

Dunnerholme

K's shoes

243

Ireleth

Hodbarrow Point

ASKAM 40¾

Askam in Furness

'pier'

ex min rly

Irish Sea

The Lots

4 BARROW 5½ Miles

self-propelled carriages fitted internally with their own diminutive steam plants) capable of seating 12 first and 36 third class passengers. The cars featured, as Furness Railway publicity hand-outs put it, "large windows affording the fullest opportunity for seeing the beautiful mountain, river and lake scenery." They were withdrawn during the First World War; perhaps the air of gaiety they tended to exude was no longer deemed suitable. Push & Pull trains took over, surviving until the unexpected announcement of the withdrawal of passenger services to Coniston in 1958. The branch was said to be losing the then considerable sum of £16,000 per annum. Though, much to local disgust, no attempt was made to introduce economies; least of all the use of more cost-effective diesel railcars. Neither was any consideration apparently given to retaining the line for summer only trains aimed at the tourist market, a possible operating compromise studiously ignored in the case of many scenic and seaside lines which underwent complete closure when summer operation and winter mothballing might have been a viable proposition. In 1962 goods traffic was taken off as well and Coniston's particularly beautiful Swiss style station demolished. A vestige of Furness Railway activity remains, however, in the shapely guise of the restored steam yacht *Gondola*, built in 1859 by the railway for use on the lake and since restored for the same purpose by the National Trust.

Its role as a junction lost, Foxfield was lucky to survive as an unstaffed halt, particularly as there is no village to speak of in the vicinity; though it does act as a railhead for the attractive little town of Broughton-in-Furness, a mile or so to the north. A good proportion of its former buildings have disappeared, not least the unusual roof which spanned the 'down' platform face, linking the also vanished goods shed with the island platform's main buildings. A water tower and the slate built station house survive, though, and the signalmen continue to work 'earlys and lates' in their timber-framed eyrie above the weatherboarded waiting shelter. It must, one imagines, be a labour of love, given the magic of the signal box's marshland setting and the comforting spirit of community prevalent amongst those who work on the Cumbrian Coast railway.

Against a backdrop of fells, the railway curves through a cutting, emerging to make a much more modest crossing of the River Duddon than was once proposed. Of all the Cumbrian Coast line's esturial encounters, its association with the Duddon seems the most mystical. The setting here calls to mind the much mourned Cornish branchline from Wadebridge to Padstow along the banks of the River Camel. The train effects a tantalising glimpse upstream towards Dunnerdale, and you find yourself longing to come back here on foot to further a more intimate relationship with this astonishingly beautiful landscape. Not that local rights of way are conducive to exploration, though an exception is the public footpath from the hamlet of Strands, through the farmyard of Low Shaw, to Lady Hall, most easily accessible from Green Road station, next stop along the line.

Sitting at home, toying with the timetable, and day-dreaming of stations yet unvisted, GREEN ROAD leaps from the page with almost poetic potential. Visions of an old drovers road winding away from a pair of isolated platforms spring to mind and prove not entirely far-fetched. Although not 'green' in the droving sense, the station does straddle a road which peters out on the nearby marsh and lies at some distance from the nearest dwelling. It is the sort of wayside halt which

might have dropped from the page of a short story by Saki, Kipling or Quiller Couch. Goodness knows how it survived Beeching, but keep its secret to yourself, Whitehall's ministry of transport mandarins would not approve.

Along the west bank of the Duddon, the line runs down to Millom. Across the estuary you can enjoy an instant replay of the route by which you journeyed up from Askam, along the coastal margin beneath the moors that separate the Duddon and Leven valleys. Homing in on Millom you might catch an unlikely glimpse of a naval frigate, or even a submarine being broken up in the sheltered anchorage of the old Borwick Rails harbour. They build them in Barrow and they come home to be broken up in Millom.

After the loneliness of Duddon Sands, MILLOM exudes a contrasting sense of humanity and activity; though not nearly so much as when the ironworks was in full swing. You need the practised eye of railway archaeologist to make out any remnants of the course of the mineral line which curved round from the main line to serve the ironworks and the vast ore mines at Hodbarrow. These undertakings generated a colossal amount of freight traffic for the Furness Railway and its successors. Each operated a stud of weird and wonderful shunting engines which, in some cases, were as old as the century when the works and the mine finally closed in 1968. Borwick Rails harbour was a hive of activity as well, handling large tonnages of imported ore from Africa and Spain. The erosion of so much heavy industry from the traffic patterns of the Cumbrian Coast railway has been devastating. As recently as 1965, 80% of the line's use was by freight as opposed to passenger train. In the same year 111 private sidings existed in the Barrow operating division of the London Midland Region of British Railways. Nowadays you could turn the first figure around and count the sidings on your fingers.

"Of all the Cumbrian Coast line's esturial encounters, its association with the Duddon seems the most mystical."

Changing direction again, the railway leaves Millom, passing the local cricket ground, and turns north-west into a flatish landscape over which their are views to the south of the coastal village of Haverigg. Nearby stands a large prison built on the site of a Second World War aerodrome, reputedly hamstrung in its operations by sand blowing off the local dunes into every conceivable crevice of the mechanisms of the planes based there. To the north the flanks of Black Combe begin to dominate the view as the railway is crossed twice by the main Millom-Whitehaven road, on both occasions at level crossings where the gates are still operated manually in the time honoured, but increasingly rare, fashion of someone emerging from the confines of a porta-cabin to open and shut them. Alongside the second level crossing stand the handsome buildings of the former Banksprings Brewery, a small independent concern owned by the Brockbank family who brewed here until the mid Fifties, making ale to serve in their chain of pubs situated throughout the West Cumberland seaboard. Soon the train is slowing for SILECROFT, another of those forgotten, back of beyond, stations which characterise the Cumbrian Coast railway.

Black & White Combes

Wainwright wrote that you could climb Black Combe in carpet slippers. For once, however, we were disinclined to take the late master fell-walker at his word, pulling on, instead, the sort of "stout walking boots" invariably recommended in outdoor magazines. Fortified, as well, by a fell-walkers breakfast, we took the train to the mellifluous station of Green Road, which turned out to be one of those enchanting wayside halts lost absolutely in the middle of nowhere. It seemed mysteriously well cared for too, and later on we discovered that a young engine driver from Barrow, together with a friend, looks after it in his spare time.

As the train echoed away into the distance, a thrush sang from the top of a neighbouring willow and the smell of cabbages wafted from a nearby field. Clusters of snowdrops lined the lane. Straight ahead sunshine bathed the russet coloured slopes of Black Combe and its lesser colleague White Combe. Here and there an isolated cloud cast a shadow on the flank of the fell, but the day was warming up and we didn't anticipate any difficulty with visibility.

Walking along minor roads through Strands and The Green was a pleasant preamble to the climb ahead. We felt like athletes limbering up for the real business of a race. A bubbling beck kept us company, chattering its way down to the estuary as if to say "I've been up yonder and it's grand!" We crossed the A5093 by the "Punchbowl Inn" and took the by-road signposted Dunningwell, turning, a hundred yards later, on to a footpath across the fields to Langthwaite Bridge.

The going was easy, one style leading to another across stone-walled pastures of cropped grass. Breasting the first rise our route lay ahead in cartographic clarity: the track up the haunch of White Combe from left to right; the traverse to the edge of Black Combe; and to the west a glimpse of the sea, and journey's end at Silecroft railway station. A pair of kissing gates led across the drive to the baronial towers of Brockwood Park, and then it was downhill to the A595, whose traffic we had to put up with for half a mile; not that it was bad, perhaps half a dozen vehicles roaring past in as many minutes.

The second footpath on the right was clearly signposted "White Combe". We turned into a deep lane between hawthorn and holly, pussy-willow and catkins, disturbing a young hawk skimming down his private thoroughfare. The coast clear, a rabbit scuttled across our path. The first few yards were squelchy, but grew drier and emerged by a pair of five-bar gates giving out on to the open fell. An old drovers road led directly upwards through the bracken like a deep scratch on a walnut cabinet. To the north-east stood the double hump top of Knott Hill. Down below lay the rim of Baystone Bank reservoir, a basin-full of gleaming water. The track grew less distinct. It was warm work, but the occasional itinerant cloud cooled us down, and we eschewed any temptation to rest.

Exactly an hour and a half after leaving Green Road station we surmounted the summit of White Combe and took a breather, availing ourselves of Kingsize Mars Bars, Seabrook Crinkle Cut Crisps, and

Barr's Irn Bru. Across the deep gulley gouged out of the fell by Whitecombe Beck stood the high screes of Black Combe's east face; a dark, melancholy side of the mountain, quite different from the sunlit slopes of bracken seen from the sea.

To reach Black Combe necessitated a detour along the ridge to the north of White Combe; level, easy walking. Soon we were turning west and ascending on a gradual incline in a south-westerly direction towards the summit of Black Combe. Below, to our left, the Duddon estuary lay mottled at low tide, patches of pale blue water strung like pearls on a necklace of creamy coloured sands. On our right the Cumbrian Coast swept northwards past the cooling towers of Calder Hall to another distant power station which we guessed was Chaplecross, on the far side of Solway Firth. We deliberately avoided looking behind us, wishing to savour the majesty of the Lakeland panorama from the very top. But it was turning into something of a race, for clouds were beginning to blow in off the sea, and we half feared that they would envelop us before we could gain the summit.

Black Combe
from White Combe

Suddenly we caught sight of two figures ahead, intruders in our pristine landscape. They must have come up from the Fell Road and been hidden from us on White Combe. It was galling to have company, however distant on a Friday in February, and now we were higher than some of the clouds billowing disconcertingly past the flanks of the fell. We pressed purposefully on, determined not to be cheated of our view from the top. Judging by Wainwright's contours, we must have been at about 1,800 feet when the first cloud wrapped us in its moisture laden shroud. A fellrunner emerged from its opacity, map around his midriff, goggles, woolly hat; the whole works. He put our puny efforts into perspective; whilst we had proudly toiled towards the top, he had run it. But then, as the actress said to the bishop, speed isn't everything. And, even better, the cloud trailed in his wake, and as he disappeared in its vapour, we could see the summit clearly ahead.

The two walkers we had seen were huddled with sandwiches in the stone windbreak, for, warm as the climb by way of White Combe had been, the west face of Black Combe was exposed to a chilly wind searing in from the sea. Turning slowly through 360 degrees, we took stock of the astonishing view. Now we could peer over Duddon to Morecambe Bay. A thin charcoal line out to sea, south of west, must, we felt, be the Isle of Man, to which ships were moving like tadpoles. Immediately below us lay a small tarn and beyond that, far far down, the coast, just in front of which the railway threaded its way through cuttings and along embankments up to Eskmeals and across the estuary at Ravenglass towards St Bees.

Finally, we turned and looked inland at the view we had been anticipating since the start of the walk. The Lakeland skyline lay clear to the east, as brightly coloured as one of those perspective relief maps the outdoor shops sell. Skiddaw, Great Gable, Scafell Pike (tinged with snow) and Helvellyn. Plus, just south of east, the unmistakeable flat top of Ingleborough, affectionately recalling our research of the Settle & Carlisle*. Wainwright dismissed the Lakeland aspect from Black Combe as "much inferior" to others, preferring to contemplate the seaward view. For us, every which way was stunning!

It had taken two and a half hours to gain the top, and we had plenty of time in hand before our homeward bound train left Silecroft. We came down from the top like gods. Nothing in the tawdry world of towns - overdrafts, poll tax arrears, red electricity reminders - could touch us. We swung down the southfacing track with a confident stride, picking out familar details: the vast flooded cavity of Hodbarrow's old iron workings; Askam's pier of slag thrusting a grey finger into the Duddon sands; the mountainous dunes of North Walney and Sandscale. A woman came jogging up the track, hot enough to have tied her jumper around her waist, and passed us with an effortless

Whicham Church

smile. Slowly we came, metaphorically and literally, down to earth; reaching the A595 by Whicham's pretty church, and took a field path to Silecroft, emerging by the plaintive war memorial. It had taken less than an hour to descend, so we walked through the village and over the railway down to the beach. Divesting ourselves of those 'stout walking boots' we tiptoed over the shingle and bathed our tired, but happy feet in the Irish Sea.

Pearson's Railway Rides: Leeds, Settle & Carlisle

Distance & Conditions
Start from Green Road station, finish at Silecroft station. OS Landranger sheet 96. Eight miles, allow four hours net walking time. Unwise to attempt in conditions of low visibility. No problems encountered underfoot.

Refreshments
Pub at The Green; pub and shop at Silecroft.

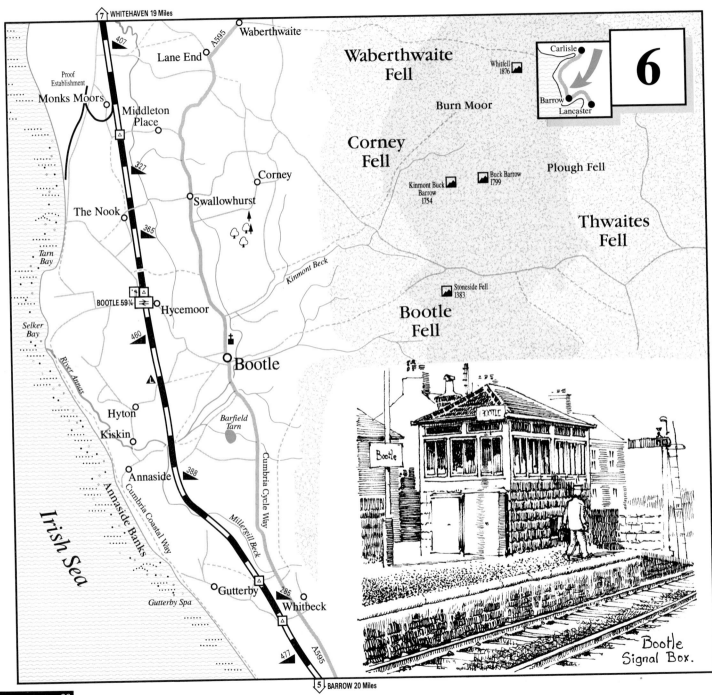

407

Waberthwaite

Lane End

A595

Proof
Establishment

Monks Moors

Middleton
Place

327

The Nook

365

Tarn
Bay

Selker
Bay

BOOTLE 59¼

Hycemoor

460

Irish Sea

Hyton

Kiskin

Annaside

388

Annaside Banks

Cumbria Coastal Way

River Annas

Waberthwaite
Fell

Whitfell
1876

Burn Moor

Corney
Fell

Corney

Swallowhurst

Kinmont Beck

Kinmont Buck
Barrow
1754

Buck Barrow
1799

Plough Fell

Thwaites
Fell

Stoneside Fell
1383

Bootle
Fell

Bootle

Barfield
Tarn

Cumbria Cycle Way

Millergill Beck

Gutterby

Gutterby Spa

Whitbeck

285

477

A595

Carlisle

Barrow

Lancaster

6

Bootle

Bootle
Signal Box.

BETWEEN Silecroft and Ravenglass the railway lies within the boundary of the Lake District National Park. Notice any change in the scenery? Well perhaps not, but at least the beauty you have already become accustomed to on your journey round the coast now has the authentic seal of approval. For a while the sea remains out of sight, and for once it is the passenger on the eastern side of the train who enjoys the better of the views. Black Combe dominates; thirty feet short of two thousand. From its summit you can see the Isle of Man, the Lakeland summits, Ingleborough, and the whole of Cumbria's nuclear coast from Heysham to Chaplecross power stations.

The line sheds some of its traffic back at Millom and this stretch of track sees only around eight passenger trains in each direction Monday to Saturday and none on Sundays. Consequently there are one or two gaps in the timetable, some of which the County Council have attempted to fill by sponsoring buses operating between stations along the line. But this comparative dearth of trains is nothing new. Skimming through old 'Bradshaws' the pattern is familiar, though there was a distinction between express and stopping trains; the former of which did not always deign to call at the likes of Silecroft or Eskmeals or Drigg. Railway timetables are an often undervalued source of information for social historians. Train times tend to reflect public demand; with the proviso that there is usually an underlying element of railway operating expediency thrown in.

If there hasn't been a great deal of change in the shape of the timetable, the shape of the trains has altered dramatically. A turn of the century Furness passenger train would have been hauled by an elegantly designed William Pettigrew (the company's chief mechanical engineer from 1897 to 1918) 4-4-0 (two driving wheels each side led by a four-wheeled bogie) built at the Glasgow works of Sharp Stewart. The train's rolling stock would be relatively plush for such a parochial line and, if they were still gas lit in 1900, within a short time they would be fitted with a form of electric lighting developed by Vickers, Maxim, the Barrow firm better known for the manufacture of machine guns! Along with the blue and white coloured carriages of the Furness Railway the train might include a crimson lake 'Midland' carriage destined for Leeds and a brown and white London & North Western to be worked through to London Euston.

The Furness Railway's motive power stud never numbered much above a hundred engines. It arguably reached its apotheosis with the introduction, in 1920, of the Rutherford designed, Kitson built 'Baltic' 4-6-4 tank engines, five massive machines of gargantuan appearence whose working life, following absorption of the Furness Railway into the L.M.S. three years later, was relatively short, the last being withdrawn in 1940. Indeed, in L.M.S. hands Furness originals were progressively replaced by standard types from the works at Crewe and Derby and only a few Furness locomotives survived into British Railways ownership, the final one, a Pettigrew 0-6-0 goods engine, being sent for scrap in 1957.

Meanwhile, those who don't give a hoot for railway history, will be watching a farming landscape swish by. A sense of loneliness and emptiness has settled on the countryside, and the railway line makes its way over embankments and through cuttings towards the next station at Bootle; more or less half way through the 120 miles between Lancaster and Carlisle. Rutted tracks lead over 'occupation' crossings and bridges to reach remote fields and outlying barns as the land spills down to the unseen sea, a strand of sand and shingle beaches usually deserted even in high summer. Gutterby Spa was a resort which never got beyond being a gleam in some optimistic Victorian entrepreneur's eye. Imagine, though, if it had, and instead of these bucolic scenes, the coastline had become a sprawl of Morecambe proportions.

British Rail's bulky timetable suffixs BOOTLE with a parenthesised Cumbria to distinguish it from the better known suburb of Liverpool. The alighting passenger could not mistake the reality of his or her destination. This Bootle is out in the wilds, a good mile's walk from the village it purports to serve, though a small community with a pub, a post office and a school has grown up beside the tracks. Date-stamped drain pipes on the station building indicate that it was built in 1873, taking the place of the original Whitehaven & Furness Junction structure following doubling of the line. Paley & Austin (lauded by Pevsner as "Lancaster's dynasty of architectures" who "large or small, could provide something personal and powerful") were given their usual architectural *carte blanche*, and the practice came up with a fanciful form of exterior walling which can only be descibed as vertical crazy paving; a *leit motif* which repeats itself in the goods shed.

> *"The land spills down to the unseen sea, a strand of sand and shingle beaches usually deserted even in high summer."*

In fact, Bootle is one of the best preserved examples of a Furness station, though, naturally, the station buildings are no longer engaged in railway duties, being, in this case, occupied residentially. On the 'down', northbound platform a trim little timber built waiting shelter adds considerable charm, enhanced by the provision of an LMS 'flowerpot'. A signal box overlooks the level crossing, whilst the goods shed has been adopted for light industrial use. Gone are the days when every railway served village had its own goods shed and a retinue of clerks and shunters employed to receive and despatch every conceivable commodity upon which the local economy depended. Perishable items would be stored in the goods shed pending collection by the local 'pick-up' goods or delivery to the consignee. For the best part of a century a village's comings and goings, its profits and losses, and the shape of its little world lay recorded for posterity in the goods clerk's leather bound ledger.

Northwards from Bootle it is still the inland fells which are likely to catch the railway traveller's eye. None aspire to the height of Black Combe, but there are some still significant, round-shouldered summits, notably Buck Barrow and Whitfell. Soon, though, the coast becomes visible again as, in the foreground, a rusty branch line loops away towards the sea, crossing a by-road into the security-fenced, watch-towered confines of the grandiloquently named Eskmeals Proof & Experimental Establishment, a Ministy of Defence armaments testing range developed on a site orignally used by Vickers for testing their big naval guns. The establishment has its own extensive network of tracks used for moving weapons into various positions for testing. They have their own locomotive (a 1956 Rushton diesel) two travelling cranes and an assortment of wagons. The internal railway is run on a daily basis, but the branch from the 'main line' is rarely used.

DUDDON SANDS

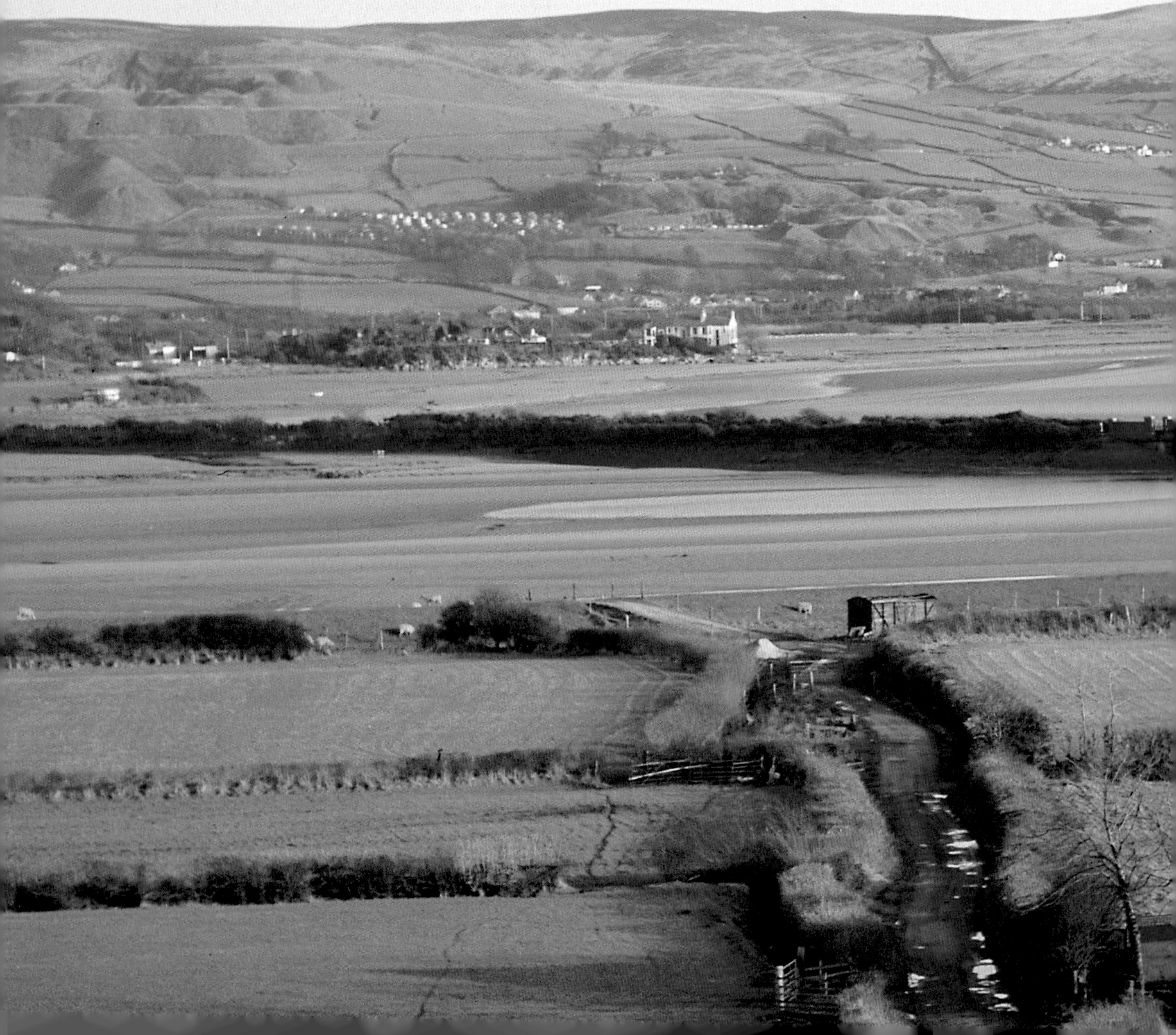

THREE rivers relinquish their individuality as they pour themselves into the Irish Sea at the ancient Roman port of Ravenglass. Irt, Mite and Esk; the last presenting the railway builders with the most formidable crossing. The first, wooden bridge was all but destroyed by fire the week before passenger trains began running in 1850. It has effectively been rebuilt three or four times and was receiving attention at the time of this guidebook's research. The tiny station of Eskmeals abutted on to the southern end of the viaduct.

Frankly, it is a toss up which way to opt to look as the train roars over the Esk. Out to sea lie the dunes of Eskmeals nature reserve. Inland extends the glorious aspect of the Esk valley, narrowing over oozy, squelchy saltings grazed by black cattle against a backdrop of Lakeland mountains; the dominant peak being Harter Fell, 2129 feet high. The Esk itself has come down from the slopes of Scafell Pike, England's highest summit; what better pedigree can a watercourse have? Approaching RAVENGLASS station, the line is carried upon an embankment above the river, and the seaward view is reminiscent of North Norfolk in general and Scolt Head in particular. Tucked beneath the inland side of the line, amongst the pine woods, are the remains of a Roman wash house, part of a fort set up here in 79BC.

Its rivers and its Romans may have moulded Ravenglass, but it is the village's association with a narrow gauge railway, affectionately referred to as 'The Ratty', which is known to a wider world. Tourists and railway lovers travel here from far and wide to sample the abundant charms of the Ravenglass & Eskdale Railway on its gorgeous journey up to Dalegarth in the depth of the hills. Always narrow gauge - but not always the same gauge - the railway was built, initially with a three feet width between the rails, in 1875 to bring haematite ore down from the mines around Boot. A couple of years after opening, it was bankrupt, but somehow or other contrived to stay in business, albeit always hovering about the edge of insolvency. Just before the Great War it was abandoned completely, and would have become just another of the forgotten mineral lines with which the western seaboard of Cumbria is littered, were it not for Bassett-Lowke, the model railway engineer, who was in search of a line on which to operate his creations. His company took over the railway in 1915 and 'halved' the gauge to 15 inches. For forty years the little railway flourished as a tourist attraction and as a general carrier of local goods, but in 1960 it was put up for sale, and only an eleventh hour rescue by a hastily convened preservation society saved it from closure again. Since then it has gone from strength to strength, establishing workshops at Ravenglass where it builds and maintains its own locomotives and rolling stock. Steam hauled trains operate most of the year round (at weekends out of season, daily during it) but there is also an early weekday morning diesel train down from Eskdale, and a corresponding teatime return working, for the benefit of local people.

At Ravenglass the British Rail and 'Ratty' stations adjoin each other and create a satisfying entity. The narrow gauge company has taken over several of the standard gauge buildings: the booking hall has become a pub called, what else, "The Ratty Arms"; the goods shed is a workshop; and the up side waiting room has been extended into a museum. Other bits and pieces of standard gauge infrastructure have been purloined: a footbridge from Coniston, canopy from Millom, and some cast iron columns from Whitehaven Bransty. Gracing the platform

are cast iron seats of Furness Railway origin, with distinctive squirrel mouldings. Only the lofty 'main line' signal box has a forlorn look about it.

The Cumbrian Coast line's second river crossing at Ravenglass is of the River Mite, an insubstantial stream which has its source up on Tongue Moor. Nearing the sea, however, it widens through a marshland landscape reminiscent of the Blyth as it nears Southwold in Suffolk; perhaps it's the narrow gauge connotation which evokes the comparison. Again the railway traveller is treated to enchanting views in either direction: the high dunes of Drigg nature reserve to the west; the splendid mountain panorama to the east. A brief interlude of fields and farms follows before the River Irt is bridged just south of Drigg. The Irt flows out of Wast Water, a beauty spot inferred in old Bradshaws as being easily accessible from Drigg station; in fact it's seven undulating miles away.

DRIGG is another classic Furness Railway station, at least on the 'up' side, where the station building now houses an interesting craft shop. "The 'down' platform, though, is bordered by security fencing and an opaque belt of conifers masking the low level disposal depot of British. Nuclear Fuels. Specially designed railway wagons are used to ferry low active waste, such as contaminated clothing and unwanted radioactive apparatus, from Sellafield to Drigg.

A lengthy cutting brings the railway to the outskirts of SEASCALE; the northbound train emerging at rooftop level to call at the windswept station of this stillborn railway inspired resort. Here the Furness Railway envisaged the growth of another 'Grange', a coastal watering place which would make money in itself as well as promoting increased rail travel. Publicity material waxed lyrical on the local climate's "noted tonic quality", drew attention to the station's "commodious refreshment rooms", and discreetly mentioned the town's newly installed sewage facilities which "are in the fore rank of modern sanitation."

The booking hall and refreshment rooms have been replaced by bus shelters, and the bare platforms are separated from the sea by a car park. Inland stands the abandoned goods yard, graced by a charmingly circular water tower and another of Paley & Austin's 'crazing paving' goods sheds, now in use as a social club. One facility the railway authorities did manage to establish was a golf links. It still flourishes, though now in the 21st century shadow of the nuclear complex of Calder Hall and Sellafield. The line runs between the links and the beach, and a palisade of sleepers tries manfully to keep sand from blowing on to the track.

Whatever your feelings concerning nuclear power, you can bet your last uranium rod, that the Cumbrian Coast railway would have been severed, north of Millom and south of Whitehaven, were it not for the presence of the nuclear industry at Sellafield. Virtually all the freight, and a good proportion of the passenger traffic, is linked, one way or another, with the BNFL plant. Slowing for SELLAFIELD station, the train crosses the River Caldew and passes exchange sidings where wagons to and from the nuclear complex are shunted into their required formations. The plant, which was developed from the 1950s onwards on the site of a Second World War ordnance factory, has its own extensive railway network. Spent uranium is transported in special safety flasks from nuclear power stations throughout Britain, and from abroad by way of Barrow docks, by rail to Sellafield for reprocessing. Sellafield reprocessing plant and Calder Hall nuclear power station

continued on page 36

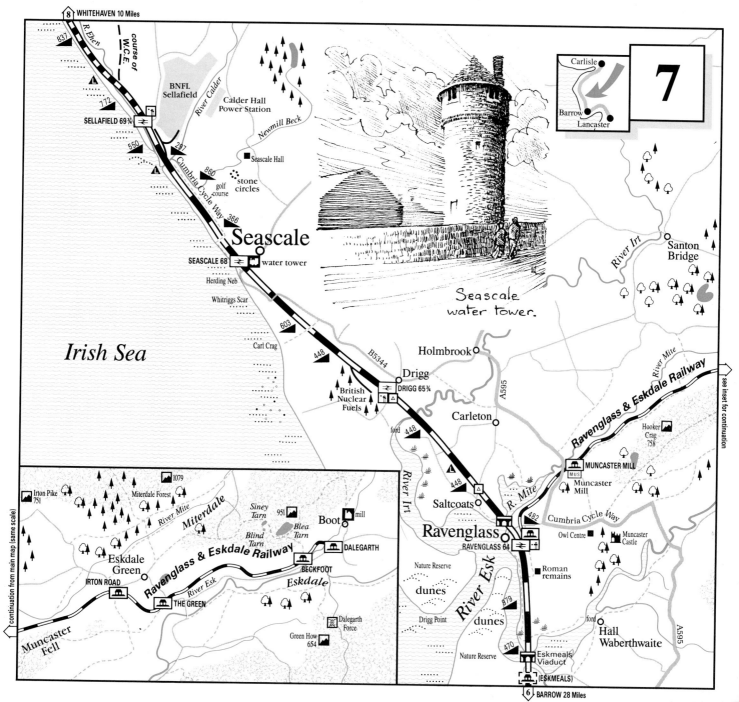

837

R. Ehen

course of W.C.E.

772

550

297

860

366

BNFL Sellafield

River Calder

Calder Hall Power Station

Newmill Beck

SELLAFIELD 69¾

Cumbria Cycle Way

Seascale Hall

stone circles

golf course

Seascale

SEASCALE 68   water tower

Herding Neb

Whitriggs Scar

603

448

Irish Sea

Carl Crag

B5344

Holmbrook

Drigg

DRIGG 65¾

British Nuclear Fuels

ford   448

448

Carleton

A595

River Irt

Santon Bridge

River Mite

Hooker Crag 758

Ravenglass & Eskdale Railway

MUNCASTER MILL
MUS
Muncaster Mill

Saltcoats

R. Mite

482

Cumbria Cycle Way

Ravenglass

RAVENGLASS 64

Owl Centre   Muncaster Castle

Roman remains

Nature Reserve

dunes

River Esk

879

dunes

Drigg Point

Nature Reserve

470

Eskmeals Viaduct

(ESKMEALS)

Hall Waberthwaite

ford

A595

see inset for continuation

Seascale water tower.

Carlisle

Barrow

Lancaster

7

Inset:

continuation from main map (same scale)

Irton Pike 751

Miterdale Forest

1079

River Mite

Miterdale

Siney Tarn

951

Blea Tarn

Blind Tarn

Boot   mill

Ravenglass & Eskdale Railway

DALEGARTH

BECKFOOT

Eskdale Green

IRTON ROAD

River Esk

THE GREEN

Eskdale

Dalegarth Force

Green How 654

Muncaster Fell

continued from page 34

occupy the same site but are essentially separate entities. For a moment or two the sea is forgotten, as the eye is drawn towards sci-fi cynosure of Sellafield.

The River Ehen flows parallel to the railway, making its way to join the sea in a manner reminiscent of the Ore in Suffolk. Sellafield station looks a bit like one of C. Reginald Dalby's illustrations from an early Rev. W. Awdry story. Perhaps this is something to do with the stark simplicity of the architecture following the station's rebuilding to

coincide with the opening of Calder Hall power station in 1956. The track layout echoes the unusual arrangement at Ulverston; this time it's the 'up' line which has the luxury of two platform faces. Water cranes recall Sellafield's lost status as a junction; a place where locomotives would run round their trains and take on water before departing whence they came, most probably inland along the now lifted tracks of the Whitehaven, Cleator & Egremont Railway.

— ❊ —

"L'al Ratty"

It was what the Scots call a 'dreich' day. Low cloud combined with a persistant drizzle made it impossible to detect where the Irish Sea ended and the Lakeland hills began. At Ravenglass the tide was out and a few scattered yachts lay beached at awkward angles like fish out of water. These were not the makings of an auspicious excursion, and prospective passengers for the noon depature to Dalegarth were thin on the ground.

The little engine left it to the last moment to pull clear of the sheds and back on to the train. It came out of the mist like a piece of Paul Daniels' magic, watched by one or two boys of all ages. Steam railways bring out the child in all of us, especially narrow guage ones like the "fifteen inch" Ratty, as the Ravenglass & Eskdale is affectionately known by its army of admirers. The engine was *Bonnie Dundee*, a sprightly 0-4-2T built to shunt in the gas works at Dundee at the turn of the century. It seems unlikely that its builders ever envisaged it running for a hundred years; still less that its latter days would be spent hauling holiday-makers up a mountainside in Cumbria.

Passenger numbers had been boosted by a few latecomers. There were two sorts of traveller. Those who ensconced themselves in the fuggy, gas warmed saloon carriages, and those who were prepared to expose themselves to the elements in one of the open sided ones. We fell into the latter category, and soon, with a sudden jolt the journey began. For the first mile, the line lay alongside the exposed mudflats of the estuary of the River Mite. Little disconsolate groups of wading birds - dunlin and redshank perhaps - stood by the waters edge. Muncaster Watermill was shut for the winter, and the train ran on into the damp woods beyond, leaving a trail of steam and smoke festooned among the overhanging branches. On the right hand side of the track the steep slope of Muncaster Fell climbed into the clouds, on the left the narrowing Mite cascaded down its course through the woods.

What fun! The carriages lurched and swayed and smoke blew back in our faces, allowing us to revel in that hot, vapoury aroma which has beguiled railway enthusiasts since Stockton & Darlington days. We

Approach to Ravenglass.

reflected that the smoothly-sprung, double-glazed class 153 diesel units, which provide such a comfortable run on the Cumbrian Coast line itself, are really the antithesis of genuine travel. Up front, with a dry, rasping chatter, *Bonnie Dundee* battled with the 1 in 48 gradient past the old quarry workings at Murthwaite which looked like a fairy grotto in the mist. We had picked up a copy of the railway's handbook. It pointed out the views we might have had if the mist had not been quite so dense. But in an odd sort of way the very lack of visibility was bringing about a deeper communion with the Ratty itself, an intimacy with the rhythm of the rail joints and the panting exertions of the diminutive locomotive at the head of the train, which, had we been oohing and ahing at the splendid scenery, we may well have overlooked.

Presently the train pulled up at a station called Irton Road, collecting a gaggle of people in Barbours and breeches. How we British love to dress up for our recreation, each form of attire being by way of a 'uniform', an indication of the 'club' to which we belong. And there is nothing so quiet as the quiet of a train that has stopped. The same silence and sense of hiatus which Edward Thomas once recognised at Adlestrop, then wrote a poem about. Away across *these* fields a distant tractor stuttered towards a misty blur of cattle with a welcome bale of winter hay.

Back along the train the guard was selling tickets to the newcomers. With a banshee wail of its whistle, *Bonnie Dundee* started back into life. More people joined the train at Eskdale Green. Then hardly had it got into its stride again, before it had to slow down and whistle stridently to effect the removal of some stray sheep from the track. After this we stopped for water, out in the wilds, by a water tank fed from the residue of water in an old mine nearby.

The last stretch of track runs alongside the road to Hardknott Pass, and we found ourselves racing a couple of cars, the occupants of which were obviously deriving more fun from seeing us than we were seeing them. Then round a sharp curve the train slowed for the Dalegarth terminus. If it had been a brighter, warmer day we would have liked to have lingered in the neighbourhood, taking a leisurely stroll up to the village of Boot to visit the inn and the Eskdale Mill. In the circumstances, though, the best we could do was spend twenty minutes thawing out in the station cafeteria before catching the return trip to Ravenglass: promising ourselves that we would come again in the summer, when all those views we had missed might be revealed.

Information

The Ravenglass & Eskdale Railway operates for much of the year, though services are restricted 'out of season'. Telephone Ravenglass (0229) 717171 for up to date timetable details. After compiling this feature it occured to us that it might have

Turnround at Ravenglass.

been more interesting to walk out from Ravenglass - across Muncaster Fell - to one of the stations along the line and return by train. A number of variations on this idea are possible and much inspiration is to be derived from Wainwright's "Walks from Ratty", a slim booklet devoted to rambling in the area which is available from the railway's ticket offices.

FROM Sellafield to St Bees the Cumbrian Coast railway runs practically along the beach. You can recognise regular travellers, as opposed to tourists, because the former are largely immune to the beauty of the view from the carriage window, whilst the latter are openly spellbound. No road could ever bring you so close to the sea for so long. For the best part of twenty minutes the trains move slowly along the coast and you can gaze across the shingle and, at low tide, the sand to where the waves of the Irish Sea are lapping the shore of England.

The tiny halts at BRAYSTONES and NETHERTOWN are as remote as anything British Rail has to offer. Access to Braystones from the outside world is restricted to a cart track. Nethertown station seems suspended between the cliff face and the sands. Either destination would offer an immediate cure for any jaded city dweller. All they would need to do is book through to either of these unfrequented stops, alight from the train, and let the seascape provide its balm.

Huddled at intervals beneath the railway embankment are the shanty homes of a community of beach-dwellers. Some of the rickety structures are occupied seasonally, a few all year round. They bear names like "Pebble Cove" and "Lobster Pot" and remind you more of the Californian world of the "Rockford Files" than anything English at all. For energy their occupants rely on generators and bottled gas.

Hard though it is to tear your eyes away from the sea, the view inland also has its enchantments. Lakeland summits like Seatallan, Haycock, Pillar and High Stile provide a contrasting vertical nobility to the horizontal lullaby of the waves. In the foreground, across the meandering Ehen, the cindery trackbed of the Whitehaven, Cleator & Egremont line heads inland. It was one of the many lines born from the discovery of rich mineral deposits in a narrow band between the Lake District mountains and the coastal plain. Scenes of Klondyke like enthusiasm prevailed and a cluster of faraway railways with strange sounding names sprang into existence to serve the mines and iron works of the area. Competition was fierce and often unprincipled; lending credence to the body of opinion which holds that were British Rail to be privatised piecemeal, chaos would ensue. Prosperity and financial hardship followed one another as local industry boomed and slumped, then boomed and slumped again. After the Depression of the Thirties, passenger trains were withdrawn from most of these lines, although workmen's services were resurrected between Moor Row, Egremont and Sellafield during the development period of the nuclear complex.

There is just time to glimpse a broad beach and craggy headland beyond before the line jerks inland, past the golf links which once had its own halt, to the station at ST BEES. Here the station building and signal box are built of sandstone: perhaps because it was easily obtained locally; perhaps in deference to the famous Elizabethan grammar school in close proximity to the line. The main station building has been converted into an attractive French restaurant, whilst the timber waiting room on the 'down' platform has become a private house.

St Bees is the only passing place on the single track section from Sellafield to Corkickle. South of St Bees trains require a 'token' to use the line. It is passed to drivers by the signalmen at St Bees or Sellafield, thereby ensuring that only one train at a time can be on the single line. Between St Bees and Corkickle protection of the single line is by the 'tokenless block' system, a modern electronic equivalent operated from the signal box.

"Scenes of Klondyke like enthusiasm prevailed and a cluster of faraway railways with strange sounding names sprang into existence."

Out over the level crossing pulls the northbound train, regaining the single track which proceeds to bisect the school playing fields occupied by young gentlemen and ladies engaged in seasonal sporting activities. This must have been a pleasantly sited school for pupils of a railway bent. One wonders what passes were inadvertently dropped, and what catches missed, with the sudden entrance into the scene of a Rutherford 'Baltic' or, towards the end of steam, a Riddles 'Britannia Pacific' on the Euston express. Today's strict diet of diesel units must seem comparatively mundane, though perhaps the Class 60 hauled coal empties from Blackburn to Maryport still stir the imagination.

The mellow valley of the Pow Beck introduces fresh scenic character to the line; presumably the watercourse was much broader in the geological past. Now the neighbouring hillsides roll steeply down to the valley floor in a scene of bucolic charm which you may well come to recall with affection as you progress though the industrial zones which lie ahead. Mirehouse Junction no longer lives up to its name. The Whitehaven Cleator & Egremont line, which climbed steeply away to scale the intervening ridge from Moor Row, remained in use for the carriage of iron ore until as recently as 1980, but now the rails are lifted, and the old trackbed exudes a similar level of melancholy to that attained by the massed ranks of the adjoining housing estate.

Near St. Bees.

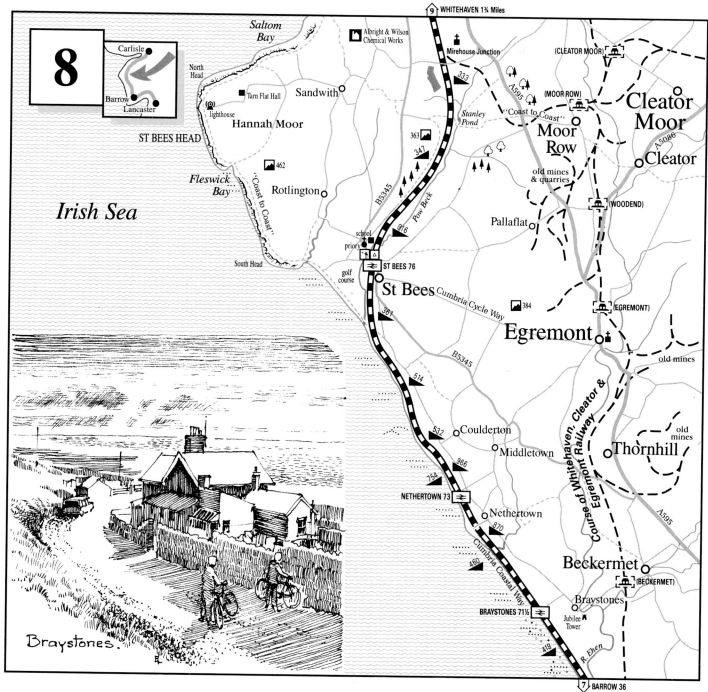

8

Carlisle
Barrow
Lancaster

Saltom Bay

Albright & Wilson Chemical Works

Mirehouse Junction

(CLEATOR MOOR)

North Head

333

A595

"Coast to Coast"

(MOOR ROW)

Tarn Flat Hall

Sandwith

Stanley Pond

Cleator Moor

363

lighthouse

Hannah Moor

347

Moor Row

Cleator

ST BEES HEAD

old mines & quarries

A5086

462

(WOODEND)

Fleswick Bay

Rotlington

B5345

Pallaflat

"Coast to Coast"

Irish Sea

Pow Beck

916

South Head

school

priory

(EGREMONT)

ST BEES 76

384

Egremont

golf course

St Bees

Cumbria Cycle Way

361

B5345

old mines

514

532

Coulderton

Middletown

old mines

966

Thornhill

754

NETHERTOWN 73

Nethertown

Course of Whitehaven, Cleator & Egremont Railway

870

A595

460

Cumbria Coastal Way

Beckermet

(BECKERMET)

BRAYSTONES 71½

Braystones

Jubilee Tower

R. Ehen

419

Braystones.

Jekyll and Hyde on the Coast

For the most part the coast of Cumbria does not flaunt itself, nor does it go in for dramtic gestures. Not for it the Flamborough Heads and Seven Sisters of other coastlines. It prefers to keep its tryst with the sea amidst a landscape of saltings and shingle. There is, though, as always, an exception which proves the rule. For at St Bees, the coast's latent exuberance gets the better of it, and the cliffs rise spectacularly about a rocky headland, three hundred and a bit feet above the thrusting waves below, from which, on a clear day, the Isle of Man can be seen.

★   ★   ★

It was one of those days when Autumn seems to have got out of the wrong side of the bed. High clouds were ballooning in off the Irish Sea like dirigibles. Workington and Whitehaven had looked at their most morose; touch flags were fluttering in the wind at St Bees School in readiness for an afternoon match, but the pitch was as yet deserted; wreaths of poppies were still strewn about the war memorial; as we headed for the sea a black-blazered boy overtook us with an urgency suggestive of an assignation, but then perhaps his coltish limbs were just glad to be free of the restraints of the classroom.

A youth in a shell suit came up from the beach looking seriously windswept. A lady with the resigned look of a house-master's wife followed with a King Charles spaniel. All the boarding houses were optimistically advertising vacancies. Behind the beach cafe the sea consumed the shingle. Turning to page three in our well-thumbed copy of Wainwright's Coast to Coast Walk, we made our way to the steps which mark the start of the epic 190 mile walk across England at the back of the lifeboat station.

In our edition (not that the author was often moved to update) Wainwright recommends keeping to the landward side of the fence which follows the clifftop. Nowadays the path is much clearer to seaward. At the top of the steps we paused to look back over St Bees, watching the waves smashing painfully against the groins. A pale, pasty faced sun struggled fitfully free from the clouds, momentarily lighting up the bulk of Black Combe to the south.

Bracken and gorse carpeted the headland. Herring gulls hung on the upwardly mobile thermals, crying their eternal sea shanty. Like Virginia Woolf, we were heading towards the lighthouse, but suddenly its white tower slipped from view as the path tumbled down to Fleswick Bay. 'A.W.' was much taken with Fleswick ("the most beautiful part of the coast") but we found it rather sullen, a gash in the headland strewn with flotsam and jetsam. The view backwards, though, as we climbed again, was astonishing, revealing the seaward side of the clifftop we had followed from St Bees in the full context of its setting. We could not, however, see anything that might possibly resemble the Isle of Man.

Soon the lighthouse came back into sight, its light signalling reassuringly out to all engaged in the maritime trade: two flashes close together followed by something like a fifteen second interval. A metalled path leads up from the clifftop to the lighthouse, so we followed it for a closer look. On weekday afternoons the keeper can, at his discretion, show members of the general public over his charge. Being a Saturday morning we didn't qualify. But having walked this far from the 'official' course of the Coast to Coast, we left 'A.W.' to ramble round the clifftop and cut inland along the Trinity House road to Sandwith.

Have you ever noticed how difficult it is to turn your back on the sea? We kept turning around to check if it was still there. Presently the road dipped and it was lost from sight. According to the map we were on Hannah Moor. Ahead of us stood Tarnflat Hall, though as we drew closer it became apparent that the 'hall' was more by way of being a farm. Hens scavenged in the not altogether prosperous looking farmyard. Suddenly, a pot bellied pig crossed our path and disappeared round the corner of the byre. West Cumbrian farming is obviously at the forefront of agricultural diversification.

Descending into Sandwith village, we briefly rejoined the route of Coast to Coasters who, can contemplate from here, the mountain

St Bees Lighthouse.

Whitehaven Harbour.

coloured earth. Over the edge of the cliffs the sea was boiling and foaming beneath an outfall pipe. Though the path seemed clear-cut on the map, there was no style in the fence bordering the field of sheep, and we had to squeeze between strands of barbed wire like a reconnaissance party in no man's land. Just, though, as we were beginning to get angry with the map, and the landowner, and the local authority, we returned, reassuringly, to a world of waymarkers and orderly styles.

The path hugged the clifftop above a rocky shore, and we headed, under the dulled gaze of grey terraced houses unlikely to be named "Sea View" or "Bosun's Locker", towards the dormant headstock of Haig Colliery whose galleries had once stretched far out beneath the sea. What a strange, surreal coast this is; one moment impeccably beautiful, the next as ugly as sin. We looked back on St Bees as one looks back on the innocence of childhood.

Out at sea a fishing smack rode the swell. We passed a coal merchant's yard fenced in like a concentration camp and came to a road not marked on the map at all. A couple were eating fish & chips in a parked car. We asked them if it led to the harbour and they nodded affirmatively between bites of batter. We strode on, racing the fishing smack to its berth, and came at length to a high bluff overlooking the port of Whitehaven, and all its piers and appurtenances. Streets of terraces petered out on the hillside. A gothic entrance lodge to a former colliery stood up gauntly like a ruined medieval watchtower. We passed an apparently inhabited house which looked like something out of the most bleak of Lowry paintings, then remembered that perhaps it was, for the artist had often been drawn to Whitehaven's seascape towards the end of his career.

The smack was embraced by the harbour's granite arms. Tight for the train, we hurried down steps and found ourselves on the periphery of the market place, busily engaged with Saturday trade. The sight of Safeways restored our bludgeoned equilibrium and we ceased to feel like characters out of a Catherine Cookson story. The walk had shown us both sides of this schizophrenic coast: its great natural beauty; its copious man-made scars. It should have been easy and obvious, but, do you know, we couldn't decide which part of the walk we had enjoyed the most!

Distance & Conditions

Start at St Bees station, finish at Whitehaven. OS Landranger sheet 89. Distance eight miles, allow three hours net walking time. Conditions good but take due care on clifftop path. The industrial half of the walk could be avoided by returning from Sandwith to St Bees via the valley of Pow Beck.

Refreshments

Refer to Gazetteer entries for St Bees and Whitehaven. There are also a couple of pubs in Sandwith.

fortress of Lakeland which lies ahead of them. Their route bore right by the "Dog & Partridge", we turned left up the lane to Town Head. At this point a change began to come over the character of the walk. A lofty concrete chimney monopolised the view. At the end of the lane we vaulted a five bar gate into a field. Two boys in cloth caps came towards us. "Did you come through Faylds?" they asked. "No, from Sandwith", we replied. They shook their heads disparagingly and passed on. None the wiser we proceeded around the perimiter fence of Albright & Wilson's vast chemical plant, until, reaching the top of the field (oh, they meant *field*, did we come through the fields!) we gained a wide view of the sea again. The same sea, but somehow different.

We slithered steeply down to a wide open space, half wasteland, half sheep pasture bisected by a path along which a man was walking a whippet towards a girl on a pony. All sorts of weird chemical smells hung in the air now that we were downwind of the works, and goodness knows what pollutants were buried beneath the stoney, bourbon biscuit

WHITEHAVEN is approached through a coppice of semaphore signals controlling movements over a rank of largely rusty sidings. Rationalisation must be too expensive, because two signal boxes remain in use, little more than a quarter of a mile apart. Between them the track briefly doubles again. On the hillside to the west a bare scar indicates the course of a rope-worked incline which wagons were worked up and down until as recently as 1986. It served Albright & Wilson's huge chemical plant at Marchon. A residue of rail traffic bound for the works is still dealt with at the nearby Preston Street goods depot, originally the terminus of the line from Barrow.

Corkickle and Bransty may sound like a couple of television detectives, but are in fact the names given to Whitehaven's two stations, though the latter name has fallen, as far as the timetable is concerned, into disuse, being known now, simply as Whitehaven. The two stations are linked, literally from platform edge to platform edge, by a single track, extraordinarily narrow and winding tunnel some three quarters of a mile in length; Whitehaven's answer to the London Underground, which takes three or four minutes to negotiate, so cautiously do the trains proceed. The year 1958 appears above the southern portal at Corkickle, referring to the completion of the tunnel's relining, a project which took thirty years! Emerging from the darkness you find yourself on a new railway, or at least the permanent way of an old one, and travelling northwards exchange the tracks of the old Furness company for those of the London & North Western Railway.

The 'Premier Line', as it liked to be known, hugs the coast from here to Maryport, but this section - originally completed as the Whitehaven Junction Railway in 1846 - was a world away in atmosphere and character from the crack service operated by the LNWR between Euston and Carlisle. This is a line of sharp, sudden curves and speed restrictions, perpetually at the mercy of stormy seas on one side and rock falls on the other. As recently as the 1960s proposals were mooted to divert trains away from this troublesome coastal line, and to run them instead inland from Sellafield, through Egremont and Moor Row to rejoin the present route at Workington; a shuttle service connecting at Moor Row for Whitehaven.

In the old days Whitehaven folk had to pass through a triumphal archway to reach Bransty station from the town centre. The station too, had an imposing air about it, its three through platforms and one bay being fully protected from the elements by canopies of iron and glass. All this was demolished in 1980 and replaced by a functional, but soul-less single storey ticket office which doesn't even run to a public toilet. Another casualty was the once extensive Harbour Commissioner's Railway whose tracks reached most of the docks, and included the steep Howgill Incline link with Haig Colliery, in use up until 1976. Antediluvian railway practice obviously survived much longer on this coast than elsewhere in the British Isles.

The Cumbrian Coast timetable expands from this point northwards to an approximately hourly service. The northern end of 'Bransty' station (the signal box still carries the old name) is characterised by scrap yards, dock silos and wastegrounds left behind by the demolition and site clearance of the old William Pit. Sidings once extended out from the mine, across the main line, and on to the shore where waste was dumped unceremoniously. One of the well known railway photographer, Colin Gifford's, most eloquent pictures showed a diminutive NCB tank

engine propelling its short train of wagons on to a trestle above the 'beach' with Whitehaven harbour and the 'Candlestick' chimney as a moody backdrop.

Candlestick chimney (once part of the hilltop Wellington Pit), the piers and their lighthouses remain, as do a stubborn pair of support columns from one of the shore sidings, and these you can glimpse as the Carlisle bound train moves slowly away from Whitehaven, picking its way gingerly along the slenderest of margins between the rocky foreshore and the high, umber coloured cliffs. This is not the seaside of the tourist brochures. Even on a fine summer day the sea seems reluctant to turn azure. This is not a shoreline likely to be considered for an EEC 'blue flag' award. Parallel to the line itself, and slightly above it, runs the course of an older waggonway which makes for an interesting walk back from Parton. Up on the headland stand the concrete remains of a second world war battery. A German submarine rose to the surface and fired on Parton during the First World War.

PARTON had railway connections even before the rails were laid along the coast, for up at the north end of the village stood the early locomotive engineering works of Messrs Tulk and Ley. The engines they built in 1840 for the Maryport & Carlisle Railway had to be sailed up the coast on giant rafts. The works, later owned by Fletcher & Jennings, and later still the Lowca Engineering Co., closed in 1912, though many of its progeny steamed on, shunting cindery industrial sidings into the 1960s. The works' site was buried beneath the spoil heaps, in their turn grassed over, of the Harrington No.10 Colliery.

From Parton a branch of the Whitehaven, Cleator & Egremont Joint Railway led inland to Distington ironworks, just one of the incredibly dense, cat's cradle network of railways which riddled this heavily industrialised district. Another line kicked back along the clifftop from Harrington, serving brick works and the aforementioned colliery, and is now an entertaining slither of the Cumbria Coastal Way.

Around Cunning Point the railway becomes single track and the embankment on the seaward side is reinforced against the violence of high 'spring' tides and on shore gales. Railwaymen know this stretch as 'Avalanche Alley'. Even on a mild day the sea can look like a particularly nasty nephew of Neptune, trying to suck the foreshore under the waves. Doubling again, the line approaches Harrington, where the curves are so tight that you don't know whether the accompanying sound effects are of the wheels squealing or the seagulls crying.

Through a gauze of smoke and steam, archive photographs of HARRINGTON reveal terraced streets, a large ironworks, and a harbour full of "salt caked smokestacks", past which the railway curves across a low viaduct into the two platformed station. Until its demise in 1930 the harbour was intensively used for the export of coal, metals (including rails from Workington) and chemicals, and the import of Baltic timber and Irish textiles. In 1899, for example, 755 vessels used the port. During the Second World War the harbour mouth was blocked and the dock adopted as a reservoir for the extraction of magnesium (used in aircraft production) from saltwater. The remains of the pumping house still dominate the pier, but in 1966 the entrance was unblocked and a new leisure role developed in Harrington harbour. There is even a sailing club, though this is not quite peaked cap, navy blazer and spotless white flannels territory. In a strange sort of way, Harrington reminded us of Sandsend on the long closed Whitby - Middlesbrough line, a location much more frequently featured in the annals of railway publishing.

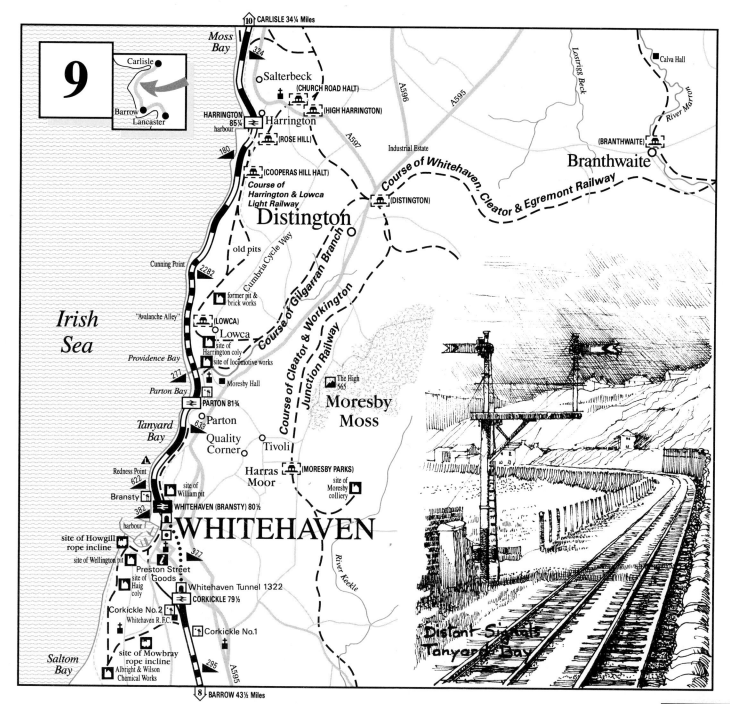

9

Carlisle
Barrow
Lancaster

10 CARLISLE 34¼ Miles

Moss Bay

324

Salterbeck

(CHURCH ROAD HALT)

(HIGH HARRINGTON)

HARRINGTON 85¼ harbour
Harrington

(ROSE HILL)

180

(COOPERAS HILL HALT)

Course of Harrington & Lowca Light Railway

old pits

Cunning Point

2282

former pit & brick works

"Avalanche Alley"

(LOWCA)

Lowca

site of Harrington coly

Providence Bay

277

site of locomotive works

Moresby Hall

Parton Bay

PARTON 81¾

Tanyard Bay

Parton

633

Quality Corner

Tivoli

Redness Point

622

Bransty

382

site of William pit

WHITEHAVEN (BRANSTY) 80½

site of Howgill rope incline

harbour

site of Wellington pit

377

Preston Street Goods

site of Haig coly

Whitehaven Tunnel 1322

Corkickle No.2

CORKICKLE 79½

Whitehaven R.F.C.

Corkickle No.1

Saltom Bay

site of Mowbray rope incline

Albright & Wilson Chemical Works

295

A595

8 BARROW 43½ Miles

Irish Sea

Distington

Industrial Estate

A596

A595

A597

Course of Whitehaven, Cleator & Egremont Railway

(DISTINGTON)

Cumbria Cycle Way

Course of Gilgarran Branch

Course of Cleator & Workington Junction Railway

Calva Hall

Lostrigg Beck

River Marron

(BRANTHWAITE)

Branthwaite

The High 565

Moresby Moss

(MORESBY PARKS)

Harras Moor

site of Moresby colliery

WHITEHAVEN

River Keekle

Distant Signals Tanyard Bay

IF YOU thought Whitehaven was 'dark' and 'satanic', Workington will only deepen your gloom, but others will respond enthusiastically to such industrial zest. From the south the railway's approach to the town is bounded by the vast - but not as vast as they were - steel works engaged in the manufacture of railway lines, both for use in Britain and throughout the world. With the perfecting of the Bessemer steel making process in the late 1860s, for which Cumbrian mined hematite was particularly suitable, two huge plants, known as the Moss Bay and Derwent Iron & Steel Works, were erected on the coastal strip below Workington. The blast furnaces remained in use until 1975, since when raw steel billets have been trained in from Teesside for rolling, forming and hardening into rails and joining, where required, into continuously welded lengths.

From the carriage window the works' sidings are a blur of yellow painted bogie bolster wagons bearing piles of orange coloured rails, and it is the walker on the adjoining Cumbrian Coastal Way footpath who has time to take in the minutae of the plant and its operations. Whatever your mode of travel, however, it is heartening to see evidence of the line being used for freight, be it the incoming billets arriving under the aegis of Rail Freight Metals from Lackenby, or the finished product preparing to depart with Civil Link. A less regularly used branch remains in situ, threading its way through the Derwent Howe Enterpise Zone (promoted to maintain the town's economy following closure of the steel making plant) to a headshunt near the harbour mouth, from which another line leads back across the river on a rickety looking trestle bridge into the dock precincts.

But let's not get bogged down with detail. The train is slowing for WORKINGTON station and there is much to look out for elsewhere. To the east, though barely to be glimpsed from the train, stand the remains of the castellated pumphouse and ornate chimney of the Jane Pit, one of several disused collieries in the town area, most of which were worked out by the end of the 19th century. This one's a must for industrial archaeology fans, being about twenty minutes walk from the station.

Once upon a time Workington had the luxury of three stations. 'Central' and 'Bridge' closed in 1931 and 1951 respectively, though the location of the former, and the associated course of the Cleator & Workington Junction Railway through the town centre can be easily traced. Workington 'Main', the station in use nowadays, has an important look about it. Its offices and waiting rooms are executed in a biscuit coloured brick more normally associated with East Anglia. Two central 'relief' lines lend an added, if now misleading sense of activity. In 1991 Workington railwaymen mourned the cessation of the celebrated Workington-Huddersfield postal train, a service with its origins back in the 1870s. Rumour had it that the authorities were going to turn out a steam locomotive for the train's final working, but in the event a grubby class 31 diesel performed the duty. Prior to the postal, Workington's most prestigious train was the "Lakes Express", which boasted alternative portions, via the coast route or along the now closed line through Keswick, which were joined at Lancaster or Crewe for the remainder of the journey to London. Nowadays posters lure Workington folk to London with reduced Apex offers, but they needs must change at Carlisle or at Lancaster to get there.

Workington harbour can be seen as northbound trains get into their stride, crossing a backwater and then the River Derwent itself;

here a blackened stream outfalling into the Irish Sea against a backdrop of derricks and oil tanks, a far cry from its idyllic origins on the eastern slopes of Great Gable in the heart of Lakeland. In the 18th century Workington docks were involved in the slave trade, but it was traditionally with the export of locally mined coal that quays were kept busy.

On the other side of the line, a glimpse of Workington Town football club emphasises the West Cumbrian affinity with the sport of rugby league. Like Barrow, Workington's soccer club has lost its league status (in this case in 1978) and so a certain local preoccupation with the oval ball game is to be expected. Indeed, throughout the Cumbrian Coast railway journey the majority of lineside playing fields sport rugby posts in winter in place of soccer goals. Workington and Barrow met in the 1955 Rugby League Cup final and British Railways ran *seventeen* special trains to carry the fans to Wembley. In those days, football, rugby, and even hockey excursions provided rich fare for train-spotters. Reporting this 1955 parade of specials along the Cumbrian Coast, "Trains Illustrated" enumerated the "Black Fives", "Jubilees" and "Patriots" which headed the trains of carousing supporters.

Just across the river you have to look closely to discern any trace of Derwent Junction and the course of the line to Cockermouth, Keswick and Penrith, a once gorgeous railway ride through the Lake District. But nearby a line does remain into the dock precincts, albeit only sporadically used. Another branch still in existence, though due for closure in 1992, leaves the main line at Siddick, providing access to a Royal Navy depot up on Broughton Moor.

Beyond Siddick the sea comes back into view, and the shore is more sandy at low tide than has been the case since St Bees. On a rough and windy day, though, high tides can spray the carriage windows. Flimby station is more exposed than most, and it pays to use the brick shelter when waiting for northbound trains, though to do so is fraught with the danger of being unseen by approaching drivers at what is usually a request stop only. Look out for the handsome sign for the adjacent "Princess Royal" pub, depicting the famous Stanier 'pacific' locomotive of the same name. At Risehow there were collieries, coke ovens and a chemical works, but all have vanished. Coal makes a comeback, however, on the outskirts of Maryport, where there is a railway loading point for opencast coal brought down by lorry from Broughton Moor. Coal trains run from here to power stations at Padiham in Lancashire and Rugeley in Staffordshire. Interestingly, the loaded wagons run by way of Shap to Padiham but along the coast route in the case of Rugeley, whilst the empties reverse the process.

MARYPORT marks the end of the Cumbrian Coast line's relationship with the sea. It is also the end of the former London & North Western Railway's territory the beginning of one of England's smallest, yet financially most resilient, railway companies, the Maryport & Carlisle. We shall enlarge upon its background as we head inland. Meanwhile, the train is coming to a halt at the curious single platform of Maryport station. Single, bi-directional platforms were a rarity in the British Isles, Cambridge being perhaps the best known example. The platform at Maryport was once occupied by the company's offices which, by all accounts, were quite palatial, given the modest size of the outfit. But this is the 1990s chum, and all that grandiloquence has given way to the functional nemesis of a glass shelter and a total absence of station staff.

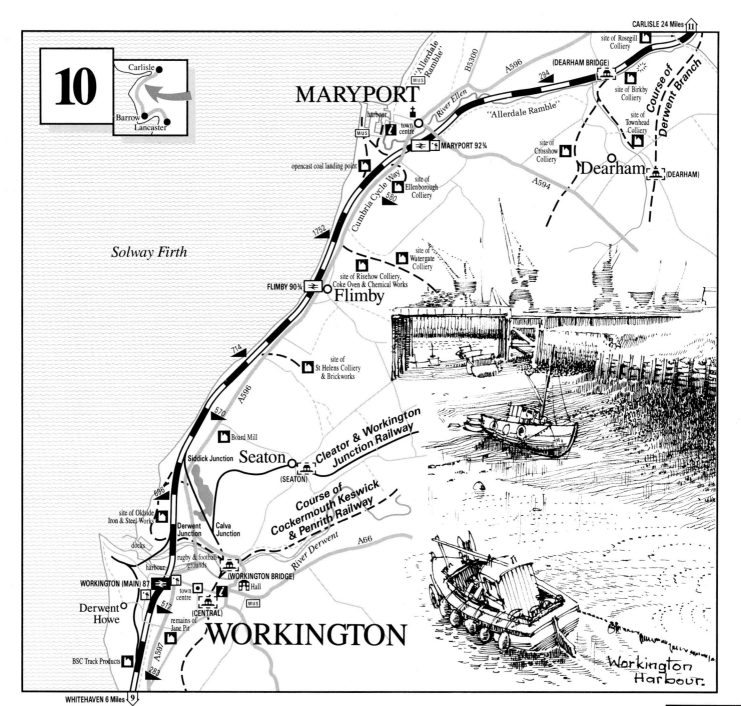

10

Carlisle
Barrow
Lancaster

CARLISLE 24 Miles [11]

site of Rosegill Colliery

B5300

A596

294

(DEARHAM BRIDGE)

site of Birkby Colliery

Course of Derwent Branch

River Ellen

"Allerdale Ramble"

site of Townhead Colliery

MARYPORT

harbour

town centre

MUS

MUS

site of Crosshow Colliery

Dearham

(DEARHAM)

A594

MARYPORT 92¾

opencast coal landing point

site of Ellenborough Colliery

580

Cumbria Cycle Way

site of Watergate Colliery

1752

Solway Firth

FLIMBY 90¾

site of Risehow Colliery, Coke Oven & Chemical Works

Flimby

714

site of St Helens Colliery & Brickworks

A596

570

Board Mill

Siddick Junction

Seaton

Cleator & Workington Junction Railway

(SEATON)

Course of Cockermouth Keswick & Penrith Railway

River Derwent

A66

696

site of Oldside Iron & Steel Works

Derwent Junction

Calva Junction

docks

rugby & football grounds

harbour

(WORKINGTON BRIDGE)

Hall

WORKINGTON (MAIN) 87

town centre

MUS

Derwent Howe

517

(CENTRAL)

remains of Jane Pit

WORKINGTON

BSC Track Products

A597

283

WHITEHAVEN 6 Miles [9]

Workington Harbour.

A little bit of the "Allerdale Ramble"

It was a Saturday in mid April and the sun was striving conscienciously to break free from a vapoury sky. We came out between the stone pillars which are all that remain of Maryport's once imposing railway station and turned right alongside the River Ellen. Daffodils waved in the riparian breeze and men were making preparations for a game of rugby league. Saturday shoppers headed for town, but we had different fish to fry, and crossed the railway before turning left on to footpath number 104044 to Dearham. In a world obsessed with numbers, is this numbering of public rights of way the thin end of a bureaucratic wedge?

Path number 104044 delved between the railway and back gardens before breaking away past building sites into fields. Reeds sighed at the edge of an inky pool. The path began to climb above the railway past hawthorn and gorse and a train wooshed by invisibly beneath the bank. After we had walked about a mile the Ellen passed beneath the railway and the path dipped down to meet it. Ahead of us an angler stalked the bank, flitting between the boles of the trees like a red indian. The river foamed prettily over a small weir and on the opposite bank, beyond the neighbouring meadow and across the railway line, stood the buildings of an old mill.

By now the path bore no comparison with its shabby beginnings, and it wound between the trees, echoing with birdsong, through a carpet of white flowering wood anemones and yellow lesser celandine. We whistled extracts from *La Boheme* and considered ourselves very lucky to have lighted upon such a paradise. Presently we came on a man cutting hazel sticks. With him was a boy of perhaps four summers wearing a bobble hat and accompanied by a mongrel. The dog leapt up on seeing us and knocked the child to the ground. "Are you alright?" we asked, helping him to his size eleven feet. "The bloody mut," said he, chuckling unconcernedly. Teach them to swear young these Cumbrians, then it's over and done with.

Beyond the wood the path turned south-eastwards away from the river and the railway, climbing through great yellow clumps of gorse which smelt like farmhouse butter freshly churned. To the east a huge spoil heap rose up against the sky at the site of Birkby Colliery. Rising through a field grazed by protective ewes with new born lambs, we reached a road junction and took the way signposted "Dearham ½". This road dropped down past the earthworks of a former mineral tramway which must have once bridged the road; turn of the century maps reveal Dearham as a community surrounded by collieries, pits and coal shafts connected to the Maryport & Carlisle Railway by a filigree of small lines. The most excitement the village could offer now was a vituperative cockerel and a vociferous cow. Even the black collie at Home Farm was too bored to bother barking.

"The Globe" had yet to open its doors to the lunchtime trade, so we turned left past the church down a track signposted with poetic simplicity "Row Brow". A youth with the physique and demeanour of Jimmy Nail in "Spender" was trying to persuade his 'marra' to take part in a forthcoming game of football, An associate lay on his back tugging at the entrails of a Ford Escort. The track swooped down to cross a swiftly flowing beck by way of a metal footbridge. Grey 'Coal Board' houses hugged the hillside and chickens roamed in a compound fenced with sheets of corrugated iron. It was noon, and somewhere over Workington way a factory siren sounded; an archaic noise seldom heard in the high-tech world of today.

The path followed the beck uphill to Row Brow, coming out on to the road by a pleasant looking pub called the "Old Mill Inn". Though

Old Railway Bridge near Rosegill.

Maryport Harbour.

The one happy memory of that lane is of its primroses, flourishing out of sight of human eyes. And eventually, like Bunyan's Pilgrim, we got free of the Slough of Despond, passing beneath a high stone haunted arch of the Derwent Branch into a mercifully dry meadow beside the railway line at Rosegill. The rusty remains of an old sluice, the broken down masonry of a weir, and the telltale shape of the adjoining house indicated that there had been a mill here at one time. In fact there were two, together with a colliery on the opposite side of the railway, though it was difficult now to picture so much activity: the churning of the waterwheels; the comings and goings at the pit head; and the snortings and pantings of passing steam trains.

We climbed the quiet lane towards Crosby, marched over its brim into the outskirts of the village and made a beeline for the bar of the "Stag Inn", downing a welcome pint of bitter before heading for the sea. By rights we should have been able to see the Scottish coast as we bowled down the hill towards Crosscanonby, but the sun was still shackled to the clouds and the sea stretched greyly out to a veiled horizon in two-tone Railfreight colours.

Crosscanonby lay demurely on the side of the hill and we paused by the lych gate of its little church. Fresh plants bloomed by the war memorial and we regarded the gravestone of one William Smith and his wife, Mary Ann, who had outlived her husband by thirty-three years; though their births had only been three years apart. The map indicated a short cut to Maryport, but we had had our fill of bridleways, and kept on the road as it descended towards Allonby Bay. The tide was out. People remained in their parked cars listening to "Sport on Five", loath to venture on to the windswept sands. The coast curved round towards Allonby like the rim of an unwashed saucer. We turned left towards Maryport.

The "Allerdale Ramble" and "Cumbria Coastal Way" shared the same path beside the golf course. On one side the beach lay sombre and devoid of people, the colour of a bruise; on the other golfers busied themselves on the greens and fairways. At the club house the path became a promenade of municipal concrete, wide and windswept and totally without hope of ever becoming as chic and as potentially popular as it must have looked on the architect's drawings long ago. We looked over the railings on to red rocks textured like waves. Then the harbour mouth came into view, its stone and timber pier jutting steadfastly out to sea as aggressively as a clenched fist. We thought of the colliers trading in and out of here during Maryport's heyday; two centuries of shipping departing heavy with Cumberland coal and iron. We felt as if we were returning from a long sea voyage ourselves. Like ancient mariners we wandered into the town on the look out for scalding hot tea and thick buttered toast. Frankly, the museums could wait for another day.

Distance & Conditions
Start and end at Maryport station, OS Landranger sheets 85 & 89. Eleven miles, allow 4 hours net. No problems other than the soggy lane to Rosegill.

Refreshments
Pub, fish & chips and general store in Dereham. Pub and post office store at Crosby. See Gazetteer for details of Maryport.

---

the hour of twelve was past, it wasn't open; obviously all day licencing hasn't percolated West Cumbria. At the far end of "The Terrace" the road rose to cross the trackbed of the old Derwent Branch railway from Bullgill to Brigham. We leant over the bridge's lichened stone parapet, trying to exorcise the present, and picture instead the passage of a Maryport & Carlisle branch line train at the turn of the century. Waving to the imaginary driver, we went on our way, jumping on to the verge to avoid a speeding van which roared past, its only occupant too busy talking into his mobile telephone to notice any pedestrians. We passed a house with an overgrown garden and then a house with a pretty one, and we continued silently along, thinking about people and their gardens, and past and present, and life and death, and whether there would be a pub open in Crosby.

By an isolated, whitewashed villa the official route of the "Allerdale Ramble" took to a metalled farm road heading south-east towards Tallentire. We kept straight on, planning to join up with the "AR's" published alternative from Tallentire to the coast below Crosscanonby. We passed the driveway to Row Hall, then New Grange farm, before turning left on to a public bridleway. It did not appear to be greatly used. The path was muddy and uneven and saplings flung their branches back in our faces. The going became difficult; more trudge than ramble. After half a mile the lane widened and passed beneath two power lines, becoming very boggy in the process. We had obviously all but pierced the water table and began to long for dry land, so that we could stride out again instead of teetering about like so many John Travoltas in platform heels.

THE SEA is just a memory. In its place the railway negotiates a landscape once desecrated by coal mining, but now reverting to its pastoral origins: grass on the spoil tips; sheep on the opencast sites. Small wonder the Maryport & Carlisle paid good dividends. A pit every mile or two; and not just on the main line. Branches struck out into the hinterland: a loop through Mealsgate, a sortie inland to Brigham and Cockermouth. Trace them on the map. But for all the long lost industrialisation, a Canadian sense of distance seems to separate each wayside community now. Vanished stations - Dearham Bridge, Bullgill, Brayton and Leegate - no longer hinder the trains; even Aspatria is only a request stop, a sombre, boarded-up effigy in railway limbo, though the recent provision of flower tubs by the local WI has brightened things up somewhat. The River Ellen, swift-flowing under antiquarian stone bridges, keeps company with the line before bending away to its source on the slopes of Skiddaw.

The Maryport & Carlisle was built on a low budget. Clearances were tight - between the running lines and beneath the bridge arches - and as a result modern Intercity rolling stock is restricted from traversing the route. When diesel multiple-units were introduced on to the line in the Fifties, they were equipped with bars over the 'drop-light' door windows to protect unsuspecting passengers from having their heads knocked-off by passing trains.

ASPATRIA station is overlooked by a large dairy, which in 1934 was the newly formed Milk Marketing Board's first factory. The new enterprise was more than a little welcome locally, for the mines in the area were in a state of decline, the last pit closing early in the war. The war brought a strange new traffic to the railway. Nearby Moota Hall became a prisoner of war camp. As many as a thousand inmates were detained at a time; Germans first, then Italians. After the war Hungarian and Lithuanian refugees were housed there. Goodness knows what the poor displaced souls made of the sombre, stone built station, drenched in soot, and the porter's profane call of "Spatry Loup Oot", roughly translated as "Change here for the Aspatria Loop."

In fact, the loop in question, a circuitous byway through the outlandishly named colliery villages of Baggrow, Mealsgate and Blaithwaite, was officially known as the Bolton Loop. It had been opened in 1866, largely to upstage a rival company's plans. A little passenger train, known colloquially as the "Baggra Bouse", shuttled back and forth between Aspatria and Mealsgate but, if Bradshaw is to believed, managed only one trip in *one* direction along the eastern end of the loop to Wigton. Real buses took over in 1930 (during the Depression the LMS took the opportunity to withdraw services from many of the more remote West Cumberland branches) and goods trains gave up the ghost in 1952, but the earthworks of the loop, named after the local parish, are still to be discerned, here and there, by those who enjoy such things.

Through woodlands of silver birch the line proceeds to the lost junction of Brayton. Carr Wood once contained a vast colliery. In utter contrast, on the other side of the tracks (literally and metaphorically) stood the demesne of Brayton Hall, home, at the turn of the century, of the Liberal member of parliament for Cockermouth, Sir Wilfred Lawson. His father had been on the board of the Maryport & Carlisle and had been provided with a private station for the estate. In time it was opened to the general public - mostly mineworkers one imagines - and remained open until 1950. Once upon a time every goods yard was home to a coal merchant who often, as is the case here, outstayed the railway. There is time, as the train hurries past, to glimpse an ornate gate lodge guarding the entrance to the driveway to the hall.

The trackbed of another long abandoned railway curves away northwards from the site of Brayton Junction. The Solway Junction Railway was a shortlived shortcut to Scotland. It was built to carry Cumberland ore to Lanarkshire ironworks, but within five years of its opening in 1869 the bottom dropped out of the market. Worse was to come. James Brunlees - engineer (remember?) of the Kent and Leven crossings - had designed a 1950 yard long, single track viaduct to carry the route across the Solway Firth. The bridge served its purpose well enough until the arctic winter of 1881, when ice floes in the firth smashed into its slender, cast iron columns, bringing great sections of the viaduct crashing down into the frozen waters. It took three years to repair the bridge, but the railway was never really the same again, apart from a brief increase of traffic during the Great War. The line closed for good in 1921, though the viaduct remained intact for another thirteen years, surreptitiously used by the locals to effect a crossing, on foot, of the firth. It was of particular use on Sundays, when by dint of a brisk mile's walk, the Scots could leave their liquor free Sabbath behind and drink to their heart's content with the Sassenachs.

Farmhouses speckle the fields, white faced like the sheep their owner's husband. In "The Kingdom by the Sea", Paul Theroux, called this surfeit of agriculture "pretty and extremely dull." The southern horizon is dominated by the three thousand foot summit of Skiddaw. The railway crosses the River Waver flowing down to the Solway Firth. Nearby an embankment overgrown with saplings masks the eastern egress of the Bolton Loop. Its trains faced a stiff 1 in 60 climb for two punishing miles from the junction. Three years after its opening in 1866, this end of the loop was dismantled through lack of use, but it was relaid in 1877 when a modicum of coal traffic developed.

They were providing a by-pass for Wigton as this guide was researched. Galling, isn't it, to be reminded of how much money the Ministry of Transport are prepared to lash out on roads? The cost of a couple of yards of tarmac would foot the bill to facelift WIGTON station, which is as down in the mouth as Dalton-in-Furness; its bus shelters frequented by adolescents, congregating here to drink and smoke and make tentatively lewd proposals to the opposite sex in the shadow of the "chemical works."

Departing past the remains of a windmill, the train dashes on towards Carlisle, making its way through a serene landscape of meadowlands bordering the River Wampool. The tall bell-tower of Highmoor Mansion, a local landmark, looms over the rooftops of Wigton. It was built by an eccentric Victorian and included a varying carillon of bells which could be heard up to a dozen miles away. The bells were dismantled after the owner went bankrupt and the mansion was subsequently converted into flats. Crofton was another initially private station. A splendid Ionic columned arch spans the driveway to the now demolished hall. On the south side of the line keep an eye open for a whitewashed farmhouse, its semi-circular walls are shaped like a fiddle and it dates from 1709.

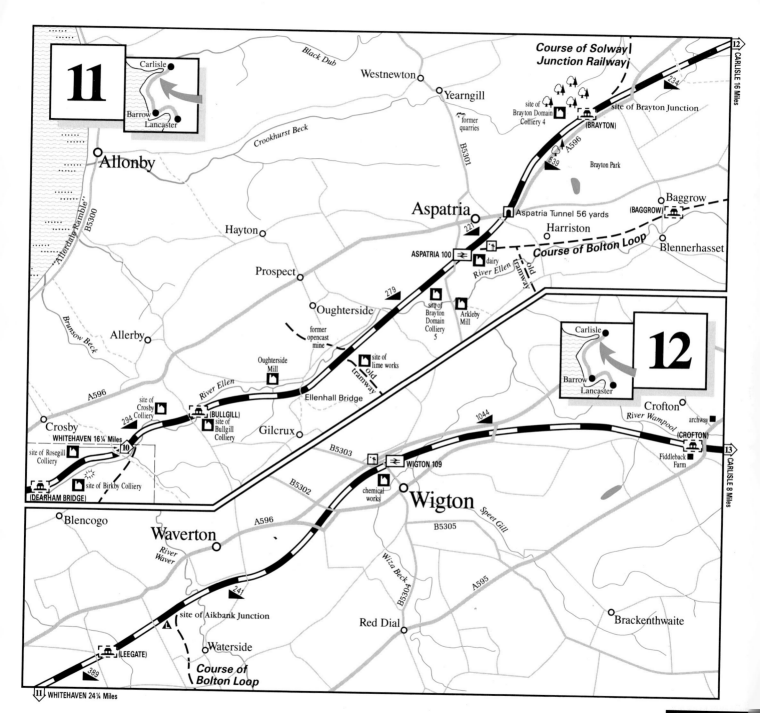

11

Carlisle

Barrow
Lancaster

12

Carlisle

Barrow
Lancaster

Black Dub

Crookhurst Beck

Westnewton

Yearngill

Course of Solway
Junction Railway

site of
Brayton Domain
Colliery 4

site of Brayton Junction

(BRAYTON)

234

CARLISLE 16 Miles

former
quarries

A596

539

Brayton Park

Baggrow

(BAGGROW)

Allonby

"Allerdale Ramble"

B5300

B5301

Hayton

Aspatria

Aspatria Tunnel 56 yards

Harriston

221

Course of Bolton Loop

Blennerhasset

Prospect

ASPATRIA 100

dairy

River Ellen

old tramway

279

Oughterside

site of
Brayton
Domain
Colliery
5

Arkleby
Mill

Brunsow Beck

Allerby

former
opencast
mine

Carlisle

12

Barrow
Lancaster

Crofton

River Wampool

archway

A596

Oughterside
Mill

site of
lime works

old tramway

(CROFTON)

13

CARLISLE 8 Miles

River Ellen

Ellenhall Bridge

Gilcrux

1044

Fiddleback
Farm

A596

site of
Crosby
Colliery

(BULLGILL)

294

site of
Bullgill
Colliery

B5303

WIGTON 109

Crosby

WHITEHAVEN 16¼ Miles

10

site of Rosegill
Colliery

site of Birkby Colliery

B5302

chemical
works

Wigton

Speet Gill

(DEARHAM BRIDGE)

Blencogo

Waverton

River
Waver

A596

B5305

Brackenthwaite

Wiza Beck

B5304

A595

Red Dial

241

site of Aikbank Junction

(LEEGATE)

389

Waterside

Course of
Bolton Loop

11 WHITEHAVEN 24¼ Miles

49

SELLAFIELD & SEASCALE

THE LAST LAP. Only the request stop at Dalston can possibly impede our sprint to the Border City. A water tower, recently restored by English Heritage, remains intact at the site of Curthwaite station. Sir Thomas (Tay Bridge) Bouch was born near here. The line snakes across a boggy area known resonantly as Cardew Mires, passes a gravel pit, then reaches DALSTON, where an oil terminal provides welcome revenue for Railfreight. Trains of oil tankers arrive here most days from either Grangemouth or Stanlow.

Dalston station lies on a curve. Its main station buildings have been partially demolished, partially converted into an engineering business. But on the 'down', Carlisle platform the attractive original waiting shelter survives, half stone, half timber, in typical Maryport & Carlisle style. Behind a screen of conifers stands the former station master's house, whilst back on the 'up' side, slightly above the station, there is a row of original railway workers' cottages. The sense of community at country stations such as this must have been very strong; very comforting to know one's 'station' in life.

The train leaves Dalston through a cutting overlooked by a Nestle's factory and emerges into the valley of the River Caldew which flows down from the eastern flank of Skiddaw. Golfers make their way around the course in the grounds of Dalston Hall with varying degrees of success; ramblers follow the "Cumbria Way"; sheep and cattle graze the meadows which can easily be subjected to flooding; and the river glides unconcernedly through its low lying valley past gorse covered banks and sandstone bluffs, with here and there an old mill to recall the days when it - like the rest of us - was more fully employed.

Just beyond the site of the old station at Cummersdale, the railway spans the river by way of a bridge of stone piers and steel girders. Hidden from view on a hillside to the east lies Carlisle Racecourse. Cummersdale station would have served the local, and quite substantial mills; still used for textile printing. The train slows, moving into the suburban fringe of Carlisle. Brick and pebble-dash semis engulf the now incongruous and compromised Georgian elegance of Currock House. Back gardens, the neat and the neglected, spill down to the lineside. Children scamper in a playground. Dogs are exercised by the riverbank. Journey's end, and a return to the mundane thread of day to day existence.

The Caldew foams and thunders over a weir by a huge and handsome mill. This was the Holme Head works of Joseph Ferguson, opened in 1824 for bleaching and dyeing, and subsequently expanded to include spinning and weaving sheds. Adjoining the mill stand neat terraced streets of employee's housing accompanied by a 'coffee house' for recreation away from the temptations of liquor. Before the advent of the railways textiles were Carlisle's stock in trade, but by the turn of the nineteenth century the railways were major employers. Seven independent railway companies forgathered in the city, each with their own engine sheds and goods yards, offices and worker's housing. Relations were not always cordial. Giuseppe Verdi could have furnished the plot for one of his operas from the arguments and counter-arguments which raged between the shifting company alliances. In 1849, with the backing of the County Sheriff, the Lancaster & Carlisle Railway engaged a gang of a hundred navvies to tear up the tracks leading to the Maryport & Carlisle's Crown Street terminus.

At Currock Junction the inbound train from the coast lurches over pointwork alongside the old Glasgow & South Western Railway's engine shed - now used for wagon storage and repair - and begins its semi-circular approach to Carlisle station. The Maryport & Carlisle's own motive power depot stood in the parcel of land, where goats now graze, between the line we are on, and the goods loop which enables through freight trains, bound south or east, to pass through the city without needing to reverse. Terraces of former railway worker's houses run down to the track as our line passes under Currock Road. One imagines returning drivers would whistle to let their womenfolk know it was time to put the tea on.

Curves don't come much tighter than the one which carries Maryport & Carlisle trains into the throat of the 'Citadel' station. This slow, wheel-squealing passage seems an appropriate coda (or overture) to the writhing and contorting that has characterised our journey. Cumbrian Coast services usually obtain a clear path into the station, and come to a halt at the bay platform traditionally assigned to Maryport & Carlisle trains. Though the name is no longer part of BR-speak, the sobriquet of 'Citadel' has applied to the city's imposing central station since it was opened in 1847.

"For nigh on a century and a half Citadel has reverberrated to the sights and sounds and smells of generations of railway activity, and it remains hugely and enjoyably redolent of the sooty spirit of the past."

Citadel by name and citadel by nature. Sir William Tite gave as scant rein to his penchant for battlements and crenellations as he had at the other end of the Lancaster & Carlisle Railway. The effect here, however, is more grandiose, and exaggerated by the huge, seven acre, train shed which still covers the greater length of the platforms, though the ornate gothic end screens were unimaginatively replaced in the Sixties. For nigh on a century and a half Citadel has reverberrated to the sights and sounds and smells of generations of railway activity, and it remains hugely and enjoyably redolent of the sooty spirit of the past. Electricity and diesel may be the prime movers now, but even without the occasional incursion of a steam special from the Settle & Carlisle line, the old ambience of the station's eclectic heyday - the Anglo-Scottish expresses pausing to change locomotives; the night mails shunting clandestinely through the small hours; the long, tired troop trains of two world wars; the Silloth locals which once steamed in along the bed of the old canal from Port Carlisle - is still tangible. And in the high-tech times which we occupy, there remains a core of railway interest - perhaps simply the shunting of a motorail van on to a southbound express - which continues to attract 'boys of all ages' out to the end of the platform.

And so here we are, a hundred and twenty miles and maybe four hours from Lancaster, at the end of our coastal railway odyssey; our imagination grappling overtime with the broad sweep and small detail of what we have seen: the estuaries, the mountains, the sea; the farms and factories. We could have taken Joseph Locke's route up over Shap and got to Carlisle in under an hour. But then the essence of real travel has no corollary with the clock, and in the words of that early railway lover, Robert Louis Stevenson, it is better to travel hopefully than to arrive.

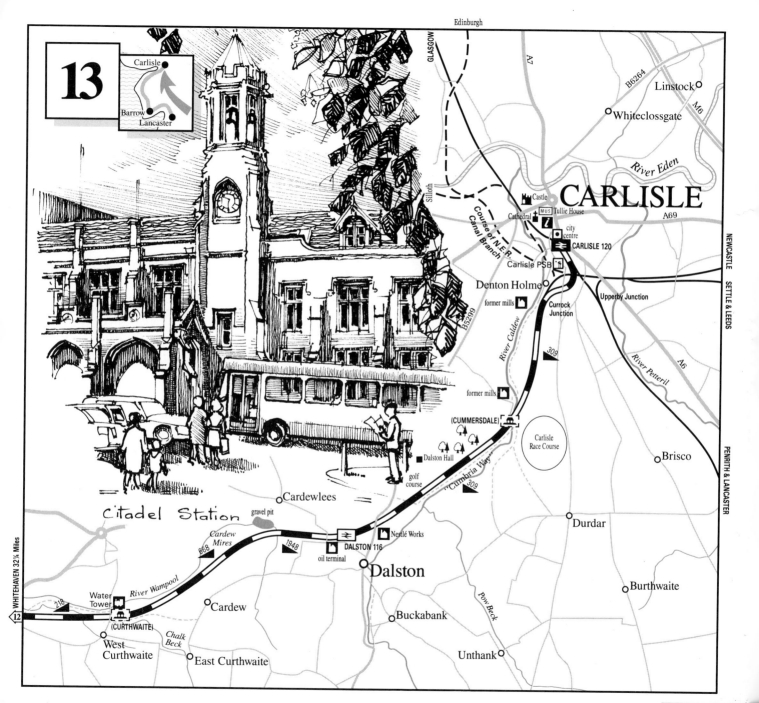

13

Carlisle
Barrow
Lancaster

Edinburgh

GLASGOW

A7

B6264

Linstock

M6

Whitecrossgate

River Eden

A69

Silloth

Course of N.E.R.
Canal Branch

■ Castle

CARLISLE

Cathedral

MUS Tullie House

i

city
centre

CARLISLE 120

Carlisle PSB

B5299

Denton Holme

former mills

River Caldew

Currock
Junction

Upperby Junction

River Petteril

A6

309

former mills

(CUMMERSDALE)

309

"Cumbria Way"

Carlisle
Race Course

■ Dalston Hall

golf
course

Brisco

Cardewlees

gravel pit

Durdar

Citadel Station

Cardew
Mires

B668

1948

oil terminal

Nestlé Works

DALSTON 116

Dalston

Burthwaite

WHITEHAVEN 32¼ Miles

River Wampool

218

Water
Tower

Cardew

Buckabank

Pow Beck

12

(CURTHWAITE)

Chalk
Beck

West
Curthwaite

East Curthwaite

Unthank

NEWCASTLE

SETTLE & LEEDS

PENRITH & LANCASTER

Gazetteer

A

Arnside

A small 'resort' of dignified villas set on a hillside overlooking the Kent estuary. The fact that it faces north probably prevented it from expanding to the size of Grange, its neighbour across the bay. Retired folk with the accents of Lancashire cotton towns sit on benches and gaze over the river towards the panorama of the Lakeland hills, and at high tide anglers fish from the pier built by the railway company to compensate for the restriction to navigation caused by construction of the viaduct. It has twice been swept away by storms. A tide table is displayed on the landward end. The incoming tide floods for about two hours before high water.

Refreshments & Accommodation.
THE PIER COTTAGE CAFE. Cosy tea room located up an alley opposite the pier; coffees, light lunches and teas.
　　YE OLDE FIGHTING COCKS. A Thwaites pub on the front near the station; bar meals and accommodation.
　　There are other cafes and pubs, together with a fish & chip shop near the station.

Shopping
Several gift shops as befits a small resort. Spar store, butcher, baker, greengrocer, newsagent, Natwest and Barclays banks.

Bus Connections
Cumberland services to/from Kendal Mon-Sat. Tel: Kendal 733221.

Things to Do
WALKING - along the course of the old railway to Sandside and back (4 miles). Or visit Arnside Knott and/or Arnside Tower (see pages 12 & 13).
　　CYCLING - hire from Arnside Pet Foods on Silverdale Road. (Phone in advance (0524) 762065).

Askam-in-Furness

Behind the terraced streets and fossilised slag-heaps of this former iron making village lies a real Copacabana of a beach, the start of a potentially marvellous six mile walk to Barrow by way of Sandscale Haws. Askam is also the finishing point of the locally promoted 'Coast to Coast' walk across Furness from Rampside. Opposite the Co-op store look out for the cast iron drinking fountain erected to commemorate Queen Victoria's Diamond Jubilee. K Shoes factory shop is open Monday to Saturday adjacent to the station. Tel: Barrow (0229) 62267.

Aspatria

A strange, straggling throwback of a town, made up of characteristically grey Cumberland buildings. The sort of place you would go to only in order to visit a distant relative or in an attempt to catch up with your past. Midland and Natwest banks, and a spattering of shops and pubs of which the best look to be BOUCH'S old fashioned general store and THE SUN INN respectively.

B

Barrow-in-Furness

Barrow reminds you of Hull. The same sense of maritime activity lurks around each terracotta corner: the dockyards; the cranes; the lunchtime surge of workers on foot which isn't seen in other industrial centres as much as it used to be. Barrow's grid-like streets are not beautiful in the generally accepted sense of the term, but have a zest about them which makes exploration more enjoyable than you would imagine. There's the unexpected dignity of the town hall of 1887, the linked squares with statues of Ramsden and Schneider, industrial Barrow's founding fathers. An altogether different Barrow exists on the far side of the Walney Channel, where the long, narrow island faces the Irish Sea along a strand of fine beaches.

Refreshments & Accommodation
ABBEY HOUSE HOTEL - Abbey Road (2 miles from station). Tel: Barrow (0229) 838282. Comfortable 'upper range' hotel housed in building designed by Lutyens. Also serve bar meals and afternoon teas and can be reached by pathway from Furness Abbey.
　　ABBEY TAVERN - Furness Abbey. Pub occupying remaining wing of former Furness Railway hotel. Nearest stations Roose or Dalton.
　　STATION BUFFET - privately operated cafe, occupying former BR refreshment rooms, which doesn't appear to have altered since the early Sixties. Good value meals and snacks in a down to earth atmosphere.
　　BECKS - take-away pies and sandwiches on Duke Street.
　　THE FERRY - Walney Promenade. Pub with steak bar overlooking Jubilee Bridge and Walney Channel.

Shopping
Town centre 5 minutes walk south-west from station. Full range of facilities; chain stores, banks etc. Market on Wed, Fri & Sat.

Things to Do
TOURIST INFORMATION CENTRE - Town Hall, Duke Street. Tel: Barrow (0229) 870156. Excellent range of local material; very helpful staff.
　　FURNESS ABBEY - see under Roose.
　　A museum devoted to Barrow's shipbuilding traditions is being developed and is expected to open during 1993/4.
　　A feature on Barrow's offshore islands appears on pages 23 & 24.

Bootle

Alongside the station there is a post office store and an inn, the STATION HOTEL, food and accommodation, Tel: Bootle (06578) 207. The village centre, a mile to east, also has a shop. There are good walks to be had along the coast in either direction, or eastwards up on to the fells.

Braystones

A remote community of beach house and static caravan dwellers, plus a spattering of houses and a folly tower commemorating Queen Victoria's diamond jubilee and the local men killed in the Great War. A mile to the east lies the attractive village of Beckermet which has two good inns (accommodation at THE WHITE MARE, Tel: Beckermet (0946) 841246) and a post office store.

C

Cark & Cartmel (& Flookburgh)

One station with two names serving three villages - confused? Well let's take them in order. To the north of the railway line lies CARK, a smallish village which grew around the site of a former mill. The pub, known as the "Engine Inn", recalls the existence of a steam pumping engine used to provide extra supplies of water to the mill. FLOOKBURGH is a quasi-picturesque fishing village with something of a 'Dutch' feel to it. The church, whose graveyard overlooks the 'switched-out' signal box, is by the ubiquitous architects Paley & Austin. Flookburgh's fishermen harvest their catches of shrimps and cockles by driving out in tractors on to the exposed sands of the Leven estuary at low tide. Nearby Ravenstown was built between the wars to provide homes for dockyard workers from Barrow. Its roads are named after First World War battles. Finally, a couple of miles to the north of the station lies the ancient and much visited centre of CARTMEL, famous for its 12th century priory and adjoining race course. The village itself is attractively laid out around an old market square.

Refreshments & Accommodation
There are pubs in Cark and Flookburgh but Cartmel offers the best choice of accommodation; try the KINGS ARMS HOTEL on Cartmel (05395) 36220.

Shopping
Cark has a post office, a Mace store and a newsagent. Flookburgh has two stores, a chemist, butcher and post office. Cartmel caters for visitors with crafts, antiques and gift shops. There are also two antiquarian bookshops, one of which, Norman Kerr, is a long established specialist in transport material.

Bus Connections
Cumberland operate a limited weekday service between Cark and Cartmel, details of which can be had on Kendal (0539) 733221.

Things to Do

Apart from the obvious lure of Cartmel (which, due to its distance from the station may be outside some people's orbit) another attraction in the vicinity is HOLKER HALL and the associated LAKELAND MOTOR MUSEUM. Both are open daily (ex Sat) from April to October. Telephone (Flookburgh (05395) 58328 for further details. Entrance to the hall is ½ mile along the B5278 north-east of Cark station.

WALKING - Potential walks from Cark station include south through Flookburgh and then west around the coastal fringe of Cartmel Sands, returning to Flookburgh via Sandgate. Alternatively walk along quiet(ish) by-roads to Cartmel, returning over the fells to the station at Grange.

Carlisle

Carlisle was always the sort of place you passed through on the way to somewhere else: generations of railway travellers were left with memories of engines being changed and wheel-tappers at work; whilst road travellers retained a blurred impression of suburban villas strung out along the A6. Nowadays, though, the 'Border City' has set out its stall as a tourist destination in its own right, somewhere capable of sustaining your interest for a day out, or as a useful base from which to explore the rich variety of landscapes that can be found on its doorstep: the Tyne Valley and Hadrian's Wall; the Eden Valley and the Pennines; the Lake District; the Cumbrian Coast of course; and the Scottish Border regions. Happily most of these areas remain served by rail, and some of the country's most scenic lines converge on the old Citadel station, which is just a moment's walk from the city centre.

Though not yet a Chester, yet alone a York, Carlisle is 'coming on nicely', and with its growing list of attractions, and increasingly prosperous and diverse shops, is a worthwhile venue on any tourist itinerary.

Refreshments & Accommodation

CUMBRIAN HOTEL - Court Square. Just outside the railway station, this is a comfortable 'three star' hotel. Tel: Carlisle (0228) 31951.

CAFE CENTRAL - Court Square. Formerly known as the 'Cumbrian Kitchen'. Handily placed beside the station for light meals and snacks.

CROWN & MITRE HOTEL - English Street. Another 'three star' hotel. Facilities include a suitably decorated 'Railway Tavern' bar. Tel: Carlisle 25491.

CATHEDRAL BUTTERY - Cathedral Close. Informal cafe for light meals, teas and coffees.

CAFE CARLYLE - Fisher Street. Attractive bistro type cafe.

Shopping

THE LANES, tucked between Scotch Street and Lowther Street, is an imaginative new shopping precinct, and there are a growing number of pedestrian courts and alleys devoted to specialist retailers, but pride of place still belongs to the COVERED MARKET, a Victorian shopping centre with architectural overtones of Citadel station itself.

Things to Do

VISITOR CENTRE - Old Town Hall, Green Market. Tel: Carlisle (0228) 512444. Admirable starting point for exploration of the city, friendly staff and wide range of leaflets and publications. Guided walks with different themes Mon-Fri throughout the summer start from here at 1.30pm lasting 1 ½ hours.

TULLIE HOUSE - Castle Street. Open daily. Currently the jewel in Carlisle's tourism crown, Tullie House features dramatic reconstructions of the city's past in a series of galleries illustrating the impact of the Romans, the Reivers and the Railways. Thoroughly recommended. Tel: Carlisle (0228) 34781.

CASTLE - Castle Way. Open daily. Well preserved fortification dating from the 11th century. Tel: Carlisle 31777.

CATHEDRAL - Castle Street. 12th century church built from red sandstone; one of the country's lesser known ecclesiastical treasures.

Bus Connections

Local route 61 is currently operated by the classic ex London 'Routemaster' half-cab design, worth hopping on for an offbeat sightseeing tour from stops beside the Citadel. Tel: Carlisle (0228) 48484.

Carnforth

A small town more notable for the routes of communication which pass through it - canal, railway and road - rather than any intrinsic value of its own.

Eating, Drinking & Accommodation

ROYAL STATION HOTEL - Market Street. Tel: Carnforth (0524) 732033. Meals and accommodation.

Shopping

Modest choice of shops. Interesting bookshop stocking new and secondhand titles. Natwest and Barclays banks.

Things to Do

STEAMTOWN. Fascinating centre for the display and maintenance of steam locomotives, rolling stock and ancillary items housed in a former motive power depot which saw use up until the end of regular steam on British Rail in 1968. Notable for its now unique coaling tower, the depot itself was built during the Second World War by Italian prisoners of war. Open daily throughout the year for the viewing of static exhibits and on special operating days for trips along a short length of line to "Crag Bank" station. There is also a 15 inch gauge minature line and an indoor model railway. For further details telephone Carnforth (0524) 732100. Entrance on Warton Road, 5 minutes walk from the station.

WALKING - to the top of Warton Crag or in either direction along the towpath of the Lancaster Canal.

Corkickle

Suburb of Whitehaven.

Dalston

The station lies out on the suburban fringe of the village, but the centre congregates around a broad square, edged by a picturesque green, starting point for riverside walks beside the Caldew. THE BLUEBELL is a comfortable country pub; next door the COUNTRY KITCHEN serves coffees, lunches and teas. Shopping facilities include a post office, patisserie, butcher, newsagent and Co-op. The "Cumbria Way" passes through Dalston and suggests an alternative approach to Carlisle; alight from the train here, and it's an enjoyable four mile walk along the bank of the Caldew into the city centre.

Dalton-in-Furness

A fiesty little town, though inclined towards shabbiness, probably as a result of its mineworking past. Deeper into history, though, it was the 'ancient capital of Furness'. Robert the Bruce raided the castle in 1322, but it is now preserved by the National Trust, and the fiercest onslaught comes from the occasional wayward tourist, intrigued enough to seek out the key from the local custodian. Shopping facilities are reasonably good (musicians should seek out 'The Violin Shop') and there's a little market on Tuesdays. Natwest and Barclays have banks in the town. For refreshments try the BROWN COW near Paley & Austin's fine parish church which includes the grave of George Romney, 18th century portrait painter. The CHEQUERS MOTEL on Abbey Road provides comfortable accommodation. Tel: Dalton (0229) 62124.

Drigg

An isolated farming village to the north of the River Irt, Drigg plays host to BNFL's low risk waste dump; though posters in local windows make it clear that there is a good deal of antipathy towards the NIREX scheme for nuclear waste to be buried locally. A road leads down to a lonely beach where you are advised to beware unexploded ammunitions, radioactive waste and poisonous snakes. The VICTORIA HOTEL (adjacent to the station) is a pleasant Jennings pub offering meals and accommodation (Tel: Holmrook (09467) 24231. The former station building houses SPINDLE CRAFT, an interesting craft shop (open daily - Tel: Holmrook 24335) specialising in knitwear, spinning wheels, and locally produced gifts.

Flimby

An old colliery village overlooking a bleak foreshore. At low tide bent figures dig for bait against a backdrop of the Galloway hills. Mary Queen of Scots is reputed to have landed hereabouts (after sailing across the Solway Firth) seeking refuge with the Curwen family of Workington Hall in 1568. Shop and pub by the station.

Foxfield

The railhead for Broughton-in-Furness, which is a pretty little town with interesting shops and pleasant inns set in streets debouching from a Georgian square.

Grange-over-Sands

"No nigger minstrels or anything of the noisy order" enthused the 1906/7 edition of the guide to 'Seaside Watering Places', and Grange is still renowned for a general disinclination to let down its hair. Year after year it attacts the sort of folk who ask nothing more of a holiday than to stroll along the promenade, to feed ducks in the park, or go in for a spot of gentle rambling on the fells behind this endearing little town. It's a sun trap too, soaking up the incandescent light of Morecambe Bay, over which the view extends to the distant coastline of Lancashire and the Pennine hills beyond.

Refreshments & Accommodation
Three stately hotels ("The Grange", "Netherwood" and "Cumbrian Grand") echo Grange's traditional appeal, and there are many smaller establishments catering for all tastes and pockets. A telephone call to the Tourist Information Centre will clarify matters. Pubs are thin on the ground, but there are some splendid tea rooms, notably HAZELMERE CAFE on Yewbarrow Terrace (just a minute's walk from the railway station) which bakes its own mouthwatering range of (eat in or take-away) savouries and pastries on the premises.
(Shop open Mon-Sat; cafe Tue-Sun).

Shopping
Grange bristles with fine individual retailers of the old school, such as Trenouth 'the complete gentlemen's outfitters', Vose the wine merchant and Ainsworth's delicatessen. All it lacks, somewhat surprisingly, is a really good bookshop; though the station newsagents - delightfully old fashioned in itself - stocks a good range of local material. There are branches of Barclays, Natwest, Midland and TSB banks.

Bus Connections
Cumberland services to/from Kendal and Cartmel. Tel: Kendal (0539) 733221.

Things to Do
TOURIST INFORMATION CENTRE - Victoria Hall, Main Street. Tel: Grange (05395) 34026. Open summer season only.
HAMPSFELL, at 727 feet the local eminence, is just a two hour round walk from the railway station where descriptive leaflets of this and other nearby walks are obtainable. For a less taxing alternative follow the promenade (and ensuing footpaths and pavements) westwards to Kents Bank station, 2 ½ level miles away.
SWIMMING - Grange's open-air, saltwater pool is located on the promenade less than 10 minutes walk from the station. Telephone the T/C to check open times and dates.
CYCLE HIRE - contact Grange Cycles on Main Street. Tel (05395) 33333.
CHILDREN'S PLAY AREA - The Promenade. Charming playground with a Furness Railway theme.
WINDERMERE BUS/BOAT LINK - mid-morning bus link from Grange Station Forecourt to Lakeside for steamer connection to Bowness. Return trip in the afternoon. Timings on Carlisle (0228) 812812.

Green Road

Splendidly isolated station, out in the wilds where Millom Marsh meets Duddon Sands. The nearest pub is THE PUNCHBOWL, a mile west at The Green. It offers food and accommodation Tel: Millom (0229) 772605. Green Road station makes a good starting (or finishing) point for an ascent of Black Combe (see feature on pages 28 & 29) or perhaps a gentler stroll along the by-roads to Millom.

Harrington

By road Harrington is little more than a contiguous suburb of Workington. By rail it seems far more individual; a little harbour almost qualifying as picturesque. Somewhat ravaged, though, it would make an admirable set for a film about the Normandy landings of 1944. Facilities on the front include a fish & chip shop and a welcoming pub called "The Ship Inn". The Cumbria Coastal Way encourages walks in either direction.

Kents Bank

Residential annex to Grange, notable for being the destination of Cross Sands guided walks from (at present, 1992) Arnside. The office of 'Guide to the Sands' is by royal appointment. The present guide, Cedric Robinson, has held the post since 1963. Like his illustrious predecessors, he lives at the Guide's Farm, Kent's Bank and can be contacted for details of forthcoming walks on Grange (05395) 32165. Facilities adjacent to the station include a post office stores, several hotels (most of which cater for non residents) and a couple of coffee shops.

Kirkby-in-Furness

Kirkby station serves a scattered neighbourhood of hamlets, some residential, like Sandside, others formerly concerned with the quarrying of slate. The Cumbria Coastal Way crosses the line at this point. THE SHIP is a friendly little 'down to earth' pub a few yards from the station but there are no longer any shops close to hand.

Lancaster

Barely a brick in sight in compact, handsome, stone built Lancaster, which was only granted city status as recently as 1937. But its pedigree goes back to the Norman Conquest, and its heyday as a Georgian port connected with the slave trade has bequeathed a legacy of elegant architecture of enduring graciousness. Trade and commerce have ebbed away from Lancaster's waterfront, but from the banks of the Lune it still looks an imposing sort of place, crowned by a skyline of turrets and battlements, domes, spires, clock towers and other miscellaneous perpendicular landmarks which provoke an urge to explore it to the full.

Refreshments & Accommodation
THE THREE MARINERS - Damside. Charming riverside pub tucked between the bus station and an animal feeds mill. Food and Lancaster brewed Mitchell's ales.
WATER WITCH - South Road. Canalside pub offering a wide range of beers (including Boddingtons) and a good menu of bar food.
ROYAL KINGS ARMS HOTEL - Market Street. Comfortable three star hotel within three minutes walk of station. Tel: Lancaster (0524) 32451.

Shopping
A good, much pedestrianised centre of shopping within easy reach of the railway station. Markets Monday - Saturday. Many characterful individual shops - look out for Atkinson's tea and coffee emporium on, appropriately enough, China Street, which looks as though only the staff have changed since it was established in 1837. Nearby stands an excellent branch of Waterstone's the booksellers.

Things to Do
TOURIST INFORMATION CENTRE - Dalton Square. Tel: Lancaster (0524) 32878.
WILLIAMSON PARK & ASHTON MEMORIAL - Lancaster's crowning glory is a folly built in 1909 in the grounds of a splendid Victorian park. It is visible for miles around (even from the station at Grange on the far side of Morecambe Bay) and reminiscent, in a vague way, of St Paul's Cathedral in London. The memorial and the grounds are open daily and attractions include a butterfly house and pavilion tea rooms. Tel: Lancaster 33318. Entrance about 1 mile east of the station.
MARITIME MUSEUM - St George's Quay. An exhibition of the Port of Lancaster housed in an elegant 18th century Custom House. Tel: Lancaster 64637. open daily (afternoons only in winter).
BUILDINGS - many of the city's most historic buildings - the castle, Catholic cathedral, old town hall

(city museum), priory and judge's lodging - are open to the public. Full details from the TIC.

PUNTING - Not quite Grantchester or the Cherwell, but much fun to be derived from hiring a punt (by the day or hour) and exploring the Lancaster Canal from Penny Street wharf. Tel: 0836 633189.

WALKING - try the "Maritime Trail". Descriptive booklets are available from various shops, museums and the TIC to this fascinating tour of Lancaster's days as an important port. The full walk will take you two or three hours to complete.

Maryport

The developers have come to town and are busy trying to turn Maryport into the St Tropez of the Cumbrian Coast. But it's an uphill task - like trying to disguise Cilla Black as Bridget Bardot - and one senses that most of the townsfolk are impervious to the planners' vision of change; the publicity shots of yachts moored beneath a Mediterranean sky don't fool them and shouldn't fool you. If, however, you strip off the cosmetics, there is more than enough character in Maryport's face (just as there is in Cilla's) to lure you into visiting this old coal port which, though it can trace its history back to Roman times, really dates from the 18th century initiative of Humphrey Senhouse who named the place after his wife.

Refreshments & Accommodation
Plenty of characterful old maritime pubs down by the harbour, but accommodation is thin on the ground; try the 'two star' WAVERLEY HOTEL adjacent to the station.

Shopping
Not yet orientated towards the tourist market, and devoid of chain stores, Maryport's shops have an old fashioned air about them. There are some especially good butchers and bakers displaying some exotic local fare well worth getting your teeth into. There are branches of Midland, Natwest and TSB banks.

Things to Do
TOURIST INFORMATION CENTRE - Senhouse Street. Tel: (0900) 813738.

MARITIME MUSEUM - as above. Cosy little exhibitions of Maryport's maritime heritage. Items devoted to local men such as Fletcher Christian (leader of the mutiny on the "Bounty") and Thomas Ismay (owner of the White Star shipping line). Nearby in the harbour, one or two steamships are on display and open at times to the general public.

SENHOUSE ROMAN MUSEUM - The Battery. Tel: (0900) 816168. Collection of antiquities unearthed locally and providing a fascinating glimpse of the Roman occupation of this area. Telephone to check opening times; small admission charge.

WALKING - Town Trail leaflets available from the TIC. Maryport lies on the route of the "Allerdale Ramble", a 55 mile walk from the heart of the Lake District to the Solway coast. See feature on pages 46 & 47.

Millom

This little town wears a brave enough smile, but since the closure of the ironworks an air of despondency stalks the tight-knit streets and there are too many solitary men of an employable age shuffling around the wastegrounds of Hodbarrow with their dogs. In essence, only those with an enthusiasm for industrial archaeology are likely to derive much enjoyment from visiting Millom, and the site of the ironworks and nearby mines exude an eerie fascination. General facilities in the town are modest, but there are branches of Barclays, Natwest and Midland banks and an adequate range of shops. The local TOURIST INFORMATION CENTRE (0229) 772555 is part of MILLOM FOLK MUSEUM, a friendly and fascinating celebration of local history featuring a reconstruction of a drift line and a typical mineworker's cottage, plus material relating to the local man of letters, Norman Nicholson.

Nethertown

A repeat performance of Braystones, right down to the beach houses and caravans. The village local is named (one senses with an air of resignation) "The Tourists".

Parton

Parton lies between its headlands like a mole on namesake Dolly's cleavage. Its houses are uniformly grey, their rendered masonry offset by brightly painted lintels and door surrounds. It is a villiage of pigeon fanciers; their lofts litter the precipitous hillside and their birds make whirlwind sorties into the Cumbrian sky. Telephone wires are strung at roof level from one side of the street to the other. A simple war memorial forms a poignant counterpoint to the station's bare platforms. The shingle beach - on which there always seems to be someone burning flotsam and jetsam - is reached through culverts in the railway embankment. Low tide exposes patches of purple coloured sand. A post office store and two pubs provide a modicum of facilities.

Ravenglass

Seagulls on the chimney pots and the dull roar of the sea beyond the high dunes characterise the old smuggling port of Ravenglass. Norman Nicholson, the local poet, called this "the most captivating village on the Lake Coast," and it would be difficult to present a considered

argument against his choice. Even without the world famous narrow gauge railway, Ravenglass has much to offer the discerning visitor, particularly if the weather is kind and he or she is the sort of person who can make their own fun, deriving enjoyment from the splendour of the village's setting at the mouth of three rivers, and not expecting a welter of tourist orientated attractions, of which there are very few.

Refreshments & Accommodation
THE RATTY - pub housed in the former Furness Railway station building and owned by the Ravenglass & Eskdale Railway. Bar meals, families welcome, cycle of guest beers and railway memorabilia.

PENNINGTON ARMS - food and accommodation. Tel: Ravenglass (0229) 717222.

Shopping
Post office stores in Main Street. Gift shop at R&ER station. Regular landings of locally caught fish.

Things to Do
TOURIST INFORMATION CENTRE - Ravenglass & Eskdale Railway station (summer only). Tel: Ravenglass (0229) 717278.

RAVENGLASS & ESKDALE RAILWAY - see feature on pages 36 & 37.

MUNCASTER CASTLE - 1 mile east of Ravenglass station. Lovely 'castle' and house dating from 13th century; 'walkman' guided tours. House open daily (ex Mon) April to October inclusive. Grounds (famed for rhododendrons and azaleas) open daily throughout the year include an Owl Centre. Refreshments available in the Stable Buttery. For further details and current admission charges telephone Ravenglass (0229) 717614 or 717203.

MUNCASTER WATER MILL - accessible from Muncaster Mill station on the Ravenglass & Eskdale Railway. Beautiful restored water mill open daily (ex Sat) throughout the summer months. Freshly milled stone-ground flour etc on sale. For further details telephone Ravenglass (0229) 717232.

'WALLS CASTLE' - local name for remains of Roman bath house, easily accessible on foot from the station.

WALKING - Ravenglass is an excellent base for walking - either inland or along the coast. Wainwright's "Walks From Ratty" booklet suggests ten mouth-wateringly splendid routes of between 2 and 7 miles length from various points along the Ravenglass & Eskdale line and can be obtained from their station shop at Ravenglass.

Roose

Nowadays a suburban conglomeration of crescents, drives, rises and avenues, but once a thriving community of Cornish miners brought in during the 1870s following the discovery of iron ore deposits at nearby Stank. Useful point to alight for a walk to FURNESS ABBEY (open daily except for winter Mondays - Tel: (0229) 23420) or along the WESTFIELD NATURE TRAIL featured on pages 23 & 24.

S

St Bees

The main part of the village struggles up a hillside half a mile from the sea. The famous boarding school, dating from 1583, lies alongside the railway, its red sandstone buildings exuding an air of well being and wisdom. Nearby, the priory church of St Bega boasts a notable Norman doorway. Down at the beach St Bees has the character of a small resort and this marks the start of Alfred Wainwright's self-styled "Coast to Coast" walk, a 190 mile trek across northern England ending up at Robin Hood's Bay on the Yorkshire coast.

Refreshments & Accommodation
FRENCH CONNECTION - attractive restaurant housed in former Furness Railway station building. Tel: St Bees (0946) 822600 for bookings and further details.

The QUEENS HOTEL (0946 822237) and MANOR HOUSE (0946 822425) both provide comfortable accommodation.

Shopping
Post office and village stores up the hill to the south-east of the station. Natwest bank open Mon, Wed & Fri. Beach cafe and shop on front.

Things to Do
Enjoy the beach and promenade or explore the coastal path around St Bees Head. See feature on pages 40 & 41.

Seascale

One of those 'if only' resorts which you come upon from time to time around the coastline of the British Isles. If only the water had been warmer; if only the view had been finer; if only the crowds had come, Seascale might have grown into another Blackpool. Instead it is a little huddle of bungalows and bay-windowed semis crouched upon a low headland overlooking a wide but featureless expanse of beach. The one row of shops (mini-market, pharmacy, newsagent, butcher, delicatessen, Midland and Natwest banks) looks wisely north away from the prevailing wind. The one hotel (THE SCAWFELL - Tel: (09467) 28400) was built in the early, heady days of optimism for the resort, and now looks reproachfully over the railway as if silently blaming it for all those untaken rooms down the years.

Sellafield

Once a remote junction station, now on the doorstep of British Nuclear Fuel's vast reprocessing and generating sites also known as Windscale and Calder Hall respectively. SELLAFIELD VISITORS CENTRE, an increasingly popular, and widely marketed attraction in the area is a bit of a trek from the station, but visitors can apply at the nearby 'main gate' of the plant for transport to the centre. Luxury 'sightseer' coaches offer visitors a guided tour of the Sellafield complex and the Visitor Centre itself displays the story of nuclear power in an imaginative series of exhibits, many of which are of a 'hands on' nature which children, in particular, will enjoy. The centre is open daily and includes a shop and restaurant. Admission is free. From time to time steam hauled excursions run to Sellafield. Further details on Seascale (09467) 27027.

Silecroft

An isolated village nestling by the foot of Black Combe. Facilities include a post office stores and an inn - THE MINERS ARMS - offering b&b, Tel: Millom (0229) 772325. Possible walking itineraries include the summit of Black Combe (see pages 28 & 29) or along the Cumbria Coastal Way. On a fine day, however, why not book through to Silecroft and simply walk down to the beach.

Silverdale

Homes for the elderly, childrens holiday camps, and caravan sites underline the inherent charms this straggling village has always held for visitors and retired folk. Cyclists and ramblers, decked out in bright colours they wouldn't be seen dead in back home, make the most of the area's contrasting attractions of coast and country.

Refreshments & Accommodation
COPPERNOBS - restaurant at Silverdale station with a railway theme. Telephone (0524) 701196 for table bookings.

In the centre of the village (a mile west of the station) there are two hotels (THE SILVERDALE and THE ROYAL) providing food and accommodation. Refreshments are also available at the RSPB visitor centre and Wolf House Gallery (see below).

Shopping
A good range of small shops (baker, chemist, grocer, newsagent, off licence, post office, co-op, delicatessen and Natwest bank 10-2.30pm) can be found in the village centre.

Things to Do
LEIGHTON MOSS - RSPB reserve and visitor centre (2 minutes walk from station; turn left and left again) open daily (ex Tue) with shop and cafeteria. Network of paths with hides for viewing birds at a discreet distance. Tel: Silverdale (0524) 701601.

WOLF HOUSE GALLERY - Restored Georgian farmbuildings converted to house craft galleries and studios. Adventure playground and refreshments. Open daily (ex Mon) from Easter to Christmas. Tel: (0524) 701405. Located about a mile south-west of Silverdale station.

WALKING - See feature on pages 12 & 13. The limestone countryside around Silverdale provides excellent walking territory and there are a number of guidebooks and leaflets detailing these available locally.

U

Ulverston

"A place where beauty, grace and cleanliness go hand in hand" is how the Furness Railway handbook of 1916 summed up Ulverston. And though we tend not to wear our hearts so transparently on our sleeves these days, it is hard to quibble with such enthusiasm. For Ulverston remains one of the most rewarding towns to visit in the whole of North-west England, all the more so as it doesn't, as yet, flaunt itself as a tourist centre. A leaflet describing local walks sums up the place admirably: "a higgledy piggledy sort of town packed into a small, sheltered space between the hills and the sea."

Refreshments & Accommodation
TRINITY HOUSE HOTEL - Princes Street. Tel: (0229) 57639. Small hotel handily placed between the station and the town.

SUN INN - Market Street. Tel: (0229) 55044. Residential free house; excellent bar lunches.

SALMONS TEA ROOMS - King Street. All day eating place.

ROSE & CROWN - convivial 'Hartleys' pub on King Street.

ULVERSTON POINT - The Gill. Bistro and cafe dealing also in crafts with a nautical flavour.

BAY HORSE - Canal Foot (1½ miles from town centre). Widely recommended pub for its food, range of beers and general ambience, idyllically located overlooking the Leven estuary. Tel: (0229) 53972.

Shopping
Much of Ulverston's charm derives from the wide variety of individual shops on display, there being a welcome dearth of chain stores. On Thursdays and Saturdays market stalls fill the narrow streets, the persuasive aroma of fish & chips being fried fills the air and the characterful market hall bustles with local folk intent on a bargain and a gossip. Two shops (among many) which caught our eye are KINGS, an excellent delicatessen on Queen Street, and FURNESS GALLERIES, a three storey treasure house of various locally produced crafts, fine arts and dolls houses; the latter made on the premises.

Things to Do
TOURIST INFORMATION CENTRE - Coronation Hall. Tel: Ulverston (0229) 57120.

LAUREL & HARDY MUSEUM - Upper Brook Street. Tel: Ulverston 52292 & 861614. Memorabilia relating to the famous Hollywood comedy duo; Stan Laurel was born in Ulverston in 1890.

CUMBRIA CRYSTAL - Lightburn Street. Tel: Ulverston 54400. Factory displays in the art of glass blowing Mondays to Fridays. Shop also open at weekends.

WALKING - Up to the 'lighthouse' on Hoad Hill or down along the old canal. See feature on pages 18 & 19. The "Cumbria Way" starts from here.

Bus Connections
Cumberland services to/from: Haverthwaite (for Lakeside

& Haverthwaite steam railway); Bowness and Windermere; Barrow via the coast (Bardsea and Roa Island). Tel: Barrow (0229) 821325.

W

Whitehaven

A grey Georgian town which mellows on acquaintance. First impressions can be off-putting, but persevere and you begin to grasp a grave, solemn beauty beneath the 'grot' and grime. Those with an interest in architecture in general and industrial archaeology in particular will soon find themselves warming to the grid-pattern streets and harbour precincts of what is claimed to be the first post-renaissance planned town in Britain. Whitehaven owed its prosperity to the importing of tobacco and the exporting of coal. At one time collieries surrounded the harbour and the seams were worked far out beneath the sea. The last pit closed in 1986, but its redundant headstock can still be seen on the hilltop to the south of the harbour. The harbour itself is only a couple of minutes walk from the station. It still supports a certain amount of trade for which the approaches are kept clear by an elderly steam powered dredger called, appropriately enough, *Clearway*. Vessels entering and leaving the harbour do so between a pair of handsome lighthouses, that on the West Pier having been designed by Sir John Rennie (son of the famous canal engineer) and erected in 1842.

Refreshments
THE GLOBE KITCHEN - Duke Street. Bustling town centre restaurant open for lunches and snacks Mon-Sat (ex Wed pm).
ARRIGHI'S - Market Place. Atmospheric fish & chip shop.

Shopping
Whitehaven's streets are full of characterful 'backstreet' shops, most notably the much publicised premises of secondhand bookseller MICHAEL MOON in Roper Street. There's a bustling market on Thursdays and Saturdays and a fair selection of the better known chain stores and banks centered on King Street and Lowther Street.

Things to Do
TOURIST INFORMATION CENTRE - Civic Hall, Lowther Street. Tel: Whitehaven (0946) 695678.

WHITEHAVEN MUSEUM - location as above. Open Mon-Sat. Small but interesting interpretation of the town's colourful past.
WALKING - clifftop walks: southwards to St Bees (see feature on pages 40 & 41) or northwards to Parton, Lowca and Harrington.

Wigton

This ancient town doesn't look its best from the railway, but once you have reached the centre, not much more than 5 minutes walk from the station, you come upon a friendly little community acting out life's rich tapestry against a backdrop of 18th and 19th century buildings which repay closer examination by the casual visitor. Armed with a Town Trail booklet (available from newsagents) offering a choice of three routes, the time between trains can be passed pleasantly and informatively. This is Melvyn Bragg's home town, and the writer and TV presenter has set a number of his novels in the area.

Refreshments & Accommodation
ROYAL OAK HOTEL - West Street. Tel: Wigton (06973) 42393. Accommodation and excellent bar and restaurant food.

Shopping
Market day on Tuesday (stalls gather round the imposing parish church of St Mary's), good range of 'small town' shops and branches of most banks.

Bus Connections
Cumberland services Mon-Sat to/from Silloth. Tel: Carlisle (0228) 48484.

Workington

Aptly named, this *is* a 'working town', and as such, unlikely to hold much appeal for the *average* tourist; not that the average tourist is likely to have delved into the esoteric charms of the Cumbrian Coast in the first place. But if you approach Workington in the right frame of mind, you may well glean some enjoyment from the experience, particularly if you progress beyond the present centre of things (a charmless void of a shopping precinct) to the gentle decaying charm of the old market place and Portland Square. In the opposite direction, west of the station, it's possible to explore the old quayside (though the still working docks on the opposite bank of the Derwent are 'out of bounds', and make your way out to the navigation light at the harbour mouth, a haunt of local fishermen, dog-walkers and those with a constitution cast-iron enough to brave the onshore breeze.

Refreshments
West of the station, salty old pubs with names like SAILORS RETURN, COASTGUARD, GEORGE IV and STEAM PACKET proliferate in backstreets by the old quay; just the thing for a maritime inspired binge.

Shopping
Good market on Weds & Sats. Town centre about ten minutes 'inland' from the station. Branches of all the main banks except for Lloyds. Wide range of shops including several chain stores.

Things to Do
TOURIST INFORMATION CENTRE - Central Car Park. Tel: Workington (0900) 602923.
WORKINGTON HALL - Hall Brow. Open daily Easter-October. Small admission charge. Tel: (0900) 604351. Handsome ruin with interpretive plaques; connections with Mary Queen of Scots.

NETHERTOWN

CUMMERSDALE & DEARHAM

Using the Cumbrian Coast Railway

Scheduled Services

Train services on the Cumbrian Coast railway are operated by Regional Railways. Modern 'Sprinter' trains provide the vast majority of services on the line, the times of which are detailed in Table 110 in British Rail's passenger timetable.

To all intents and purposes the route is divided into three distinct sections: Lancaster-Barrow; Barrow-Whitehaven; and Whitehaven-Carlisle. Services in the first and last instances are fairly frequent on Mondays to Saturdays but more restricted, particularly between Whitehaven and Carlisle, on Sundays. A less dense, but still fairly regular service operates between Barrow and Millom - with some extensions to Sellafield - from Monday through to Saturday, but there is no Sunday service on this section. The most sparsely served length of the line is between Sellafield and Whitehaven which currently (1992) has five trains in each direction Monday to Saturday.

The whole of the Cumbrian Coast timetable was re-cast in 1992 and considerably improved in the process. The current service structure makes imaginative and practical use of the line's rolling stock resources, offering through travellers, and those journeying to and from specific destinations as well, a good choice of trains at realistic intervals. If any criticism could be made, it is the absence during the summer season of Sunday trains on the central section of the line. The days when people tended not to travel on The Sabbath are long gone. Indeed, on many roads Sunday is the busiest day for traffic as town and city dwellers make for the countryside and the coast. Venues such as Ravenglass, Sellafield and St Bees would benefit greatly from the provision of public transport on a Sunday.

The average time for a through journey along the whole 120 miles of the Cumbrian Coast railway between Lancaster and Carlisle is four or five hours depending on whether or not (and it usually is) it is necessary to change at Barrow. It is not practical to list departure times in a publication of this nature as these are likely to change during the currency of this guide. However, pocket timetables are published by Regional Railways for the whole of the Cumbrian Coast line and these are widely available from staffed stations and some Tourist Information Centres in the region. Timetable information can also be obtained by telephone from the stations at Lancaster (0524) 32333; Barrow (0229) 820805; and Carlisle (0228) 44711.

Tickets

For short journeys between stations on the Cumbrian Coast line, single or day return tickets are ideal. Fuller exploration of the railway can be made with a 'Day Ranger' (£10.50 in 1992) which offers unlimited travel between Lancaster and Carlisle via the coast by any train on Saturdays and Bank Holidays or after 8.30am on Mondays to Fridays. For longer periods in the vicinity, a North-West Rover allows you to select either 3 days from a period of 7 on which to enjoy unlimited travel or a full 7 day version is also available; ideal if you are spending a week's holiday in the area. Only Standard Class accommodation is provided on Cumbrian Coast scheduled services. Further details of ticketing are obtainable from British Rail travel centres and the staffed stations at Lancaster, Grange, Ulverston, Barrow, Whitehaven, Workington and Carlisle. Passengers joining trains at these stations should purchase their tickets before boarding their train. Other stations on the Cumbrian Coast line are unstaffed and tickets must be purchased on the train.

Bicycles

Bicycles are carried free of charge on most Cumbrian Coast line services, though on 'Sprinter' trains the space available is restricted. On one or two peak hour services a reservation must be made in advance for the carriage of a bicycle. Further details are available in the leaflet "The Rail Travellers Guide to Biking By Train" available from all British Rail stations.

Charter Trains

The following organisations occasionally operate excursions - some steam hauled - along the Cumbrian Coast railway.

Intercity - Tel: London 071-388 0519
Flying Scotsman Services -
Tel: Lichfield (0543) 419472
Hertfordshire Rail Tours - Tel: Welwyn (043871) 5050
Steamtown ("Furness Flyer" Shuttles) -
Tel: Carnforth (0524) 732100

Useful Contacts

Cumbrian Railways Association - an enthusiasts group formed in 1976 to further interest in the railways of the county. Current membership secretary is G. Holme, 1 Thurlow Way, Barrow-in-Furness, Cumbria LA14 5XP

Transport Users Consultative Committee - body for dealing with complaints or comments regarding services on the Cumbrian Coast line which Regional Railways are unable to deal adequately or appropriately with. Contact: The Secretary, Transport Users Consultative Committee, Room 112, Boulton House, 17-21 Chorlton Street, Manchester M1 3HY.

Cumbria Tourist Board - Tel: (05394) 44444.

Cumbria County Council "Travel-Link". Bus and train timing details on Carlisle (0228) 812 812.

Steam Operations - "Steamline", a recorded telephone service, gives details of steam excursion dates and timings (useful for photographers). Tel: 0898 88 1968.

Weathercall - Cumbria & Lake District - 0891 500 719.

Uncaptioned photographs
Front Cover: Parton Bay
Rear Cover: "Furness Flyer" and Barrow Monument
Frontispiece: Kent Viaduct, Arnside
This page: "John Logie Baird" with coal empties